Math

Grade 3

Table of Contents

P9-AGI-593

Table of Contents

CREDITS

Concept Development: Kent Publishing Services, Inc.
Written by: Dawn Purney
Editor: Carla Hamaguchi
Designer/Production: Moonhee Pak/Carrie Carter
Illustrator: Jenny Campbell
Art Director: Tom Cochrane
Project Director: Carolea Williams

© 2004 Creative Teaching Press, Inc., Huntington Beach, CA 92649
Reproduction of activities in any manner for use in the classroom and not for commercial sale is permissible.
Reproduction of these materials for an entire school or for a school system is strictly prohibited.

Introduction

The Advantage Math Series for grades 3–6 offers instruction and practice for key skills in each math strand recommended by the National Council for Teachers of Mathematics (NCTM), including

- numeration and number theory
- operations
- geometry
- measurement
- patterns, functions, and algebra
- data analysis and probability
- problem solving

Take a look at all the advantages this math series offers . . .

Strong Skill Instruction

- The **teaching component** at the top of the activity pages provides the support students need to work through the book independently.

- Plenty of **skill practice** pages will ensure students master essential math computation skills they need to increase their math fluency.

- A **problem-solving strand** is woven within skill practice pages to offer students an opportunity to practice critical thinking skills.

teaching component

skill practice

problem solving

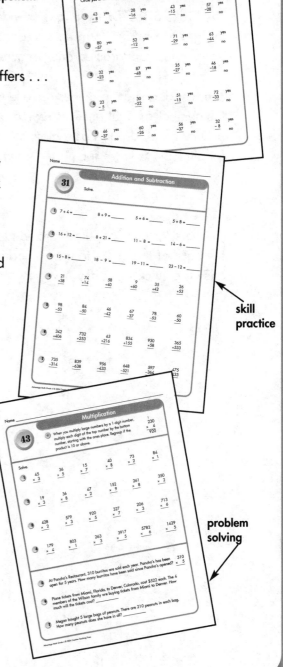

- **Mixed-practice pages** include a variety of math concepts on one workbook page. This challenges students to think through each problem rather than rely on a predictable format.

Assessment

- The "Take a Test Drive" pages provide practice using a **test-taking** format such as those included in national standardized and proficiency tests.

- The **tracking sheet** provides a place to record the number of right answers scored on each activity page. Use this as a motivational tool for students to strive for 100% accuracy.

Answer Key

- Answers for each page are provided at the back of the books to make **checking answers quick and easy.**

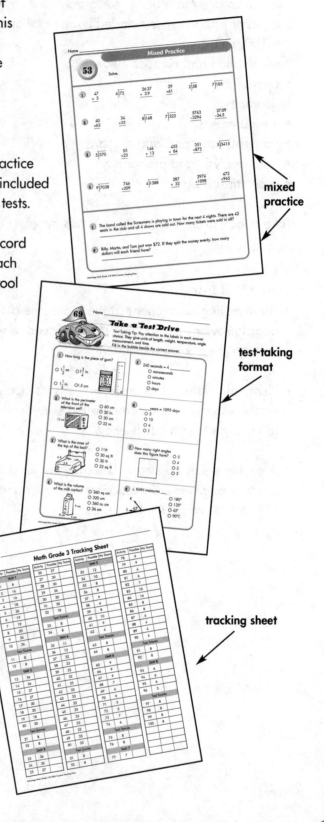

mixed practice

test-taking format

tracking sheet

Name _____

Place Value

1

⭐ The place where a digit appears in a number determines its value.

hundred   tens   ones

142 = 1 hundred 4 tens 2 ones

Write how many hundreds, tens, and ones in each number.

1   236 ____ ____ ____
                                              hundreds tens ones

2   409 ____ ____ ____
                                              hundreds tens ones

3   84 ____ ____ ____
                                              hundreds tens ones

4   350 ____ ____ ____
                                              hundreds tens ones

Write the number.

5   _____

6   _____

7 5 hundreds, 7 tens, 6 ones   _____

8 3 hundreds, 2 tens   _____

Place Value

2

Write the number.

1. 3 thousands, 4 hundreds, 5 ones   3,405

2. 2 thousands, 6 hundreds, 2 ones   _____

3. 5 thousands, 2 hundreds, 6 tens, 4 ones   _____

4. 7 thousands, 9 hundreds, 3 tens   _____

5. eight thousand, three hundred, forty   _____

6. six thousand, fifty-three   _____

7. 5 hundred, eighty-one   _____

8. 6 thousand, 4 hundred, twenty-one   _____

9. 10 more than 465   475

10. 100 more than 1,909   _____

11. 1 less than 1,439   _____

12. 50 less than 552   _____

13. 100 less than 3,542   _____

14. 10 more than 704   _____

15. 1,000 more than 643   _____

16. 1,000 less than 1,411   _____

Expanded Form

3

⭐ 2,971 = 2,000 + 900 + 70 + 1   350 = 300 + 50

2,971 and 350 are written in **standard form.**
2,000 + 900 + 70 + 1 and 300 + 50 are written in **expanded form.**

Write the number in standard form.

1 7,000 + 400 + 80 + 3 = _____   400 + 60 + 1 = _____

2 400 + 30 + 5 = _____   3,000 + 200 + 20 + 7 = _____

3 600 + 30 + 1 = _____   4,000 + 60 + 8 = _____

4 5,000 + 400 + 7 = _____   100 + 20 + 2 = _____

5 8,000 + 100 + 60 + 7 = _____   700 + 6 = _____

6 4,000 + 200 + 30 = _____   4,000 + 400 = _____

Write the number in expanded form.

7 1,863 = _____

8 942 = _____

9 4,730 = _____

10 5,072 = _____

Expanded Form

4

Write the number in expanded form.

1 14,367 = _____

2 9,208 = _____

3 1,029 = _____

4 594 = _____

Get Ahead

Write one digit in each square to complete the cross-number puzzle.

Across
A. 5,000 + 300 + 20 + 1
C. ninety-three
E. 4 thousands, 3 hundreds, 6 tens, 7 ones
G. 10 less than 169
I. 9,000 + 200
J. 4 tens
K. 6,000 + 700 + 3

Down
A. 50 + 8
B. one hundred ninety-three
D. 3 thousands, 6 hundreds, 1 ten
E. 100 more than 342
F. 7 tens, 5 ones
H. 1 more than 946
I. 900 + 6

Rounding

5

⭐ When you round a number to the nearest 10, think first about what 10 comes before and after the number.

16 is between 10 and 20. 16 rounds up to 20.

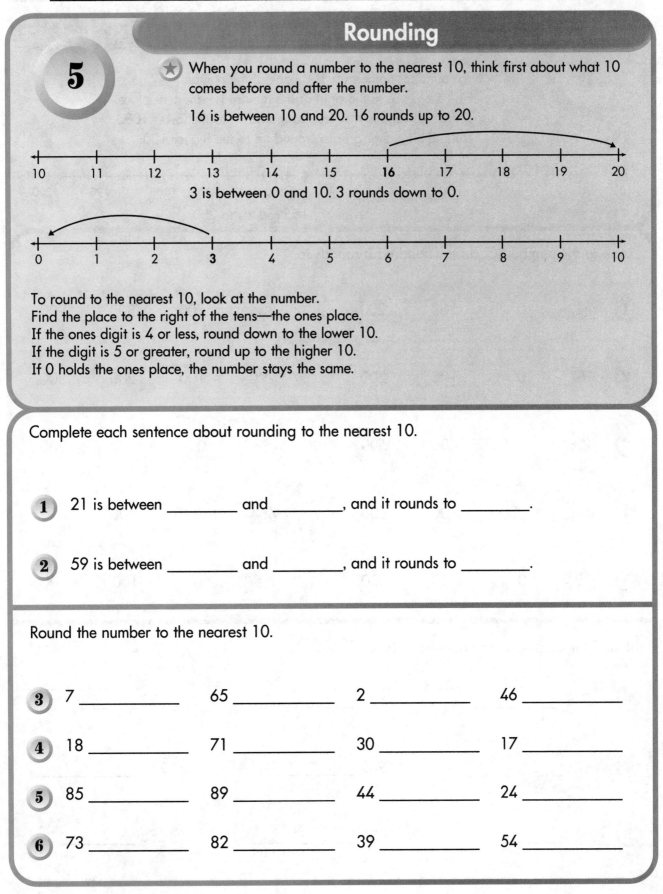

3 is between 0 and 10. 3 rounds down to 0.

To round to the nearest 10, look at the number.
Find the place to the right of the tens—the ones place.
If the ones digit is 4 or less, round down to the lower 10.
If the digit is 5 or greater, round up to the higher 10.
If 0 holds the ones place, the number stays the same.

Complete each sentence about rounding to the nearest 10.

1 21 is between _____ and _____, and it rounds to _____.

2 59 is between _____ and _____, and it rounds to _____.

Round the number to the nearest 10.

3 7 _____   65 _____   2 _____   46 _____

4 18 _____   71 _____   30 _____   17 _____

5 85 _____   89 _____   44 _____   24 _____

6 73 _____   82 _____   39 _____   54 _____

Rounding

6

⭐ To round to the nearest 100, look at the number.
Find the place to the right of the hundreds—the tens place.
If the tens digit is 4 or less, round down to the lower 100.
If the digit is 5 or greater, round up to the higher 100.

```
├┼┼┼┼┼┼┼┼┼┼┼┼┼┼┼┼┼┼┼┼┼┼┼┼┼┼┼┼┼┼┼┼┼┼┼┼┼┼┼┼┼┼┼┼┼┼┼┼┼┼┤
100   110   120   130   140   150   160   170   180   190   200
```
155 rounds to 200

Look at the number. Circle the hundred it rounds to.

1 129   0   100   200   835   700   800   900

2 187   0   100   200   290   100   200   300

3 408   300   400   500   38   0   100   200

4 372   300   400   500   464   400   500   600

5 150   0   100   200   55   0   100   200

Round the number to the nearest 100.

6 518 _____   850 _____   423 _____

7 675 _____   949 _____   764 _____

8 64 _____   302 _____   288 _____

Rounding

7

⭐ To round to the nearest 1000, look at the number.
Find the place to the right of the thousands—the hundreds place.
If the hundreds digit is 4 or less, round down to the lower 1000.
If the digit is 5 or greater, round up to the higher 1000.

| 3000 | 3100 | 3200 | 3300 | 3400 | 3500 | 3600 | 3700 | 3800 | 3900 | 4000 |

3230 rounds to 3000

Look at the number. Underline the digit in the hundreds place. Circle the thousand it rounds to.

1. **3400**   2000   3000   4000   **8935**   7000   8000   9000

2. **1587**   0   1000   2000   **2490**   1000   2000   3000

3. **2408**   2000   3000   4000   **532**   0   1000   2000

4. **5372**   5000   6000   7000   **464**   0   1000   2000

5. **4850**   4000   5000   6000   **1092**   0   1000   2000

Round the number to the nearest 1,000.

6. 3,457 _____   8,329 _____   5,907 _____

7. 1,056 _____   2,530 _____   843 _____

8. 2,944 _____   3,939 _____   6,500 _____

Name _____

Rounding

8

⭐ When rounding a number to the nearest 10, the number in the hundreds place usually stays the same. 238 rounded to the nearest 10 is 240. The hundreds place will only change if the nearest 10 is a 100. 197 rounded to the nearest 10 is 200.

Complete each sentence about rounding to the nearest 10.

1 343 is between ___340___ and _____, and it rounds to _____.

2 695 is between _____ and _____, and it rounds to _____.

Round the number to the nearest 10.

3 487 _____   95 _____   120 _____

4 986 _____   145 _____   695 _____

⭐ When rounding a number to the nearest 100, the number in the thousands place usually stays the same. 1,239 rounded to the nearest 100 is 1,200. The thousands will only change if the nearest 100 is a 1,000. 2,980 rounded to the nearest 100 is 3,000.

Round the number to the nearest 100.

5 1,360 _____   6,006 _____   8,039 _____

6 7,638 _____   7,089 _____   4,782 _____

7 3,807 _____   8,377 _____   2,360 _____

8 4,562 _____   9,923 _____   5,444 _____

Name _____

Order Numbers

9

⭐ When you put numbers in order, you compare them.

= means "is equal to"
$5 = 2 + 3$ 5 is equal to 2 plus 3

< means "is less than"
$5 < 6$ 5 is less than 6

> means "is greater than"
$5 > 4$ 5 is greater than 4

When comparing 2-digit numbers, look at the tens place first. $31 > 29$
31 is greater than 29 because the 3 in the tens place is greater than the 2 in the tens place.

Write the symbol that completes the number sentence.

1 9 _____ 6   19 _____ 22   8 _____ 13

2 25 _____ 40   7 _____ 3 + 4   37 _____ 41

3 2 + 5 _____ 9   35 _____ 45   62 _____ 61

4 8 _____ 11   64 _____ 98   17 _____ 8 + 9

5 60 _____ 6   87 _____ 78   36 _____ 63

6 1 + 6 _____ 7   54 _____ 45   9 _____ 6 + 6

7 45 _____ 52   48 _____ 47   11 _____ 21

8 50 _____ 40   7 + 6 _____ 13   96 _____ 78

Name _____

10

⭐ When comparing 3-digit numbers, look at the hundreds place first.

603 > 589

603 is greater than 589 because the 6 in the hundreds place is greater than the 5 in the hundreds place. If the digits in the hundreds place are equal, compare the digits in the tens place, and so on.

= equals
< is less than
> is greater than

Write the symbol that completes the number sentence.

1. 100 _____ 300   50 _____ 5   90 _____ 900

2. 100 + 200 _____ 300   143 _____ 201   624 _____ 480

3. 749 _____ 293   287 _____ 215   164 _____ 167

4. 589 _____ 59   873 _____ 892   342 _____ 343

5. 101 _____ 97   51 + 51 _____ 100   452 _____ 437

Complete the number sentence so that it is true. Hint: There is more than one correct answer for each one.

6. 24 = _____   432 > _____   63 < _____

7. 317 < _____   272 = _____   958 = _____

8. 469 = _____   835 > _____   416 > _____

Name _____

Take a Test Drive

Fill in the bubble beside the correct answer.

1 Which number has 3 hundreds, 2 tens, and 5 ones?
- ○ 523
- ○ 235
- ○ 352
- ○ 325

2 How many hundreds, tens, and ones does the number 703 have?
- ○ 7 hundreds, 3 tens, no ones
- ○ 7 hundreds, no tens, 3 ones
- ○ 3 hundreds, 7 tens, no ones
- ○ 3 hundreds, no tens, 7 ones

3 Which number has 5 thousands, 8 hundreds, and 6 tens?
- ○ 685
- ○ 586
- ○ 5,860
- ○ 5,608

4 Which number is the standard form for 300 + 70 + 9?
- ○ 3,079
- ○ 379
- ○ 3 hundreds, 7 tens, 9 ones
- ○ three hundred, seventy-nine

5 Which number is equal to 2,000 + 50 + 6?
- ○ 256
- ○ 652
- ○ 2,506
- ○ 2,056

6 Which expanded number is equal to 4,850?
- ○ 4 + 8 + 5 + 0
- ○ 400 + 80 + 50
- ○ 400 + 800 + 50
- ○ 4,000 + 800 + 50

7 What is 25 rounded to the nearest 10?
- ○ 20
- ○ 26
- ○ 30
- ○ 40

8 What is 25 rounded to the nearest 100?
- ○ 0
- ○ 20
- ○ 100
- ○ 200

Take a Test Drive

Fill in the bubble beside the correct answer.

1 What is 548 rounded to the nearest hundred?
- ○ 500
- ○ 540
- ○ 550
- ○ 600

2 What is 548 rounded to the nearest ten?
- ○ 500
- ○ 540
- ○ 550
- ○ 600

3 What is 3,602 rounded to the nearest thousand?
- ○ 3,000
- ○ 3,600
- ○ 3,700
- ○ 4,000

4 What is 3,602 rounded to the nearest hundred?
- ○ 3,000
- ○ 3,600
- ○ 3,610
- ○ 3,620

5 What is 596 rounded to the nearest ten?
- ○ 580
- ○ 590
- ○ 600
- ○ 1,000

6 Which symbol completes the number sentence? 31 _____ 270
- ○ =
- ○ <
- ○ >
- ○ +

7 Which number completes the number sentence? 463 > _____
- ○ 643
- ○ 464
- ○ 364
- ○ 1,400

8 Which symbol completes the number sentence? 687 _____ 678
- ○ =
- ○ <
- ○ >
- ○ +

Addition—Mental Math

13

Add. Memorize these basic facts. Learn them by heart.

1) $4 + 5 =$ _____ $5 + 6 =$ _____ $8 + 6 =$ _____ $9 + 4 =$ _____

2) $8 + 7 =$ _____ $9 + 5 =$ _____ $6 + 9 =$ _____ $4 + 8 =$ _____

3) $7 + 7 =$ _____ $7 + 9 =$ _____ $8 + 8 =$ _____ $5 + 5 =$ _____

4)
$$\begin{array}{cccccc} 7 & 9 & 10 & 5 & 5 & 6 \\ +6 & +8 & +\,4 & +4 & +8 & +6 \\ \hline \end{array}$$

5)
$$\begin{array}{cccccc} 7 & 6 & 4 & 9 & 4 & 5 \\ +8 & +4 & +9 & +6 & +6 & +9 \\ \hline \end{array}$$

6)
$$\begin{array}{cccccc} 4 & 6 & 5 & 8 & 6 & 4 \\ +7 & +8 & +7 & +5 & +5 & +4 \\ \hline \end{array}$$

7)
$$\begin{array}{cccccc} 8 & 8 & 7 & 9 & 7 & 9 \\ +4 & +9 & +4 & +7 & +5 & +9 \\ \hline \end{array}$$

Name _____

14

Add. Memorize the basic facts. Learn them by heart.

1 $3 + 7 =$ _____ $2 + 6 =$ _____ $10 + 8 =$ _____ $12 + 4 =$ _____

2 $2 + 5 =$ _____ $11 + 3 =$ _____ $4 + 3 =$ _____ $10 + 7 =$ _____

3 $12 + 2 =$ _____ $2 + 9 =$ _____ $11 + 8 =$ _____ $3 + 6 =$ _____

4
$$\begin{array}{r} 6 \\ +2 \\ \hline \end{array} \qquad \begin{array}{r} 3 \\ +9 \\ \hline \end{array} \qquad \begin{array}{r} 12 \\ +5 \\ \hline \end{array} \qquad \begin{array}{r} 10 \\ +4 \\ \hline \end{array} \qquad \begin{array}{r} 5 \\ +8 \\ \hline \end{array} \qquad \begin{array}{r} 11 \\ +4 \\ \hline \end{array}$$

5
$$\begin{array}{r} 12 \\ +6 \\ \hline \end{array} \qquad \begin{array}{r} 5 \\ +3 \\ \hline \end{array} \qquad \begin{array}{r} 10 \\ +6 \\ \hline \end{array} \qquad \begin{array}{r} 8 \\ +2 \\ \hline \end{array} \qquad \begin{array}{r} 10 \\ +2 \\ \hline \end{array} \qquad \begin{array}{r} 8 \\ +3 \\ \hline \end{array}$$

6
$$\begin{array}{r} 10 \\ +5 \\ \hline \end{array} \qquad \begin{array}{r} 10 \\ +3 \\ \hline \end{array} \qquad \begin{array}{r} 11 \\ +7 \\ \hline \end{array} \qquad \begin{array}{r} 12 \\ +8 \\ \hline \end{array} \qquad \begin{array}{r} 7 \\ +3 \\ \hline \end{array} \qquad \begin{array}{r} 11 \\ +2 \\ \hline \end{array}$$

7
$$\begin{array}{r} 12 \\ +7 \\ \hline \end{array} \qquad \begin{array}{r} 9 \\ +3 \\ \hline \end{array} \qquad \begin{array}{r} 11 \\ +5 \\ \hline \end{array} \qquad \begin{array}{r} 10 \\ +7 \\ \hline \end{array} \qquad \begin{array}{r} 9 \\ +2 \\ \hline \end{array} \qquad \begin{array}{r} 12 \\ +3 \\ \hline \end{array}$$

Addition—No Regrouping

15

⭐ When you find a sum, add the digits in the ones place first. Then add the digits in the tens place.

```
  52        5 2        5 2       52
+47       +4 7       +4 7      +47
            9         9 9       99
```

Solve.

1
```
  34        26        39        46        37        68
+25       +42       +60       + 3       +52       +21
```

2
```
  24        17        82        30        19        50
+63       +42       + 5       +67       +60       +21
```

3
```
  59        48        25        33        17        66
+20       +41       +62       +64       +51       +13
```

4
```
  45        63        74        82        11        25
+44       +25       +11       +13       +64       +62
```

5 Miss Quinn's class of 25 students has recess with Mrs. Santoso's class of 31 students. How many students have recess together? _____

6 Jacob and his dad put a vegetable tray together for a party. They cut 36 celery sticks and 42 carrot sticks. How many vegetable sticks did they cut altogether?

_____

7 It is 14 miles from home to the mall and another 23 miles to the skating rink. How many miles is it from home to the skating rink by way of the mall? _____

Addition—No Regrouping

16

⭐ When you find a sum, add the digits in the ones place first. Then add the digits in the tens place. Finally, add the digits in the hundreds place.

hundreds tens ones	hundreds tens ones	hundreds tens ones	
153 +234	153 +234	153 +234	153 +234	153 +234
	7	87	387	387

Solve.

1)

| 334 +205 | 290 +507 | 573 +326 | 183 + 13 | 836 +102 | 372 + 25 |

2)

| 94 +403 | 621 + 7 | 423 + 61 | 550 +439 | 685 +114 | 701 + 86 |

3)

| 267 + 20 | 800 +161 | 418 +250 | 614 +203 | 777 + 12 | 249 +610 |

4)

| 173 +521 | 607 +242 | 363 +404 | 174 +800 | 542 +232 | 156 +441 |

5) All 75 third graders put on a play for the 223 students in the lower grades. How many students were at the play altogether? _____

6) Sam had 145 cards in his collection. His sister Jane had 214. How many did they have in all? _____

7) Casey's classroom library had 325 books. Ellie's mom donated 62 more books to the library. How many books were in the library altogether? _____

Addition—Regrouping

17

⭐ When adding, look at the ones column first. Can you make a group of ten from the ones? If you can, regroup.

Add the ones.

```
  tens  ones
   1
    2    6
 +  5    8
 _____
         4
```

Are there ten or more after adding the ones? Yes. 6 + 8 = 14. You can regroup by writing a 1 in the tens column. Write the 4 below the line in the ones column.

Add the tens.

```
  tens  ones
   1
    2    6
 +  5    8
 _____
    8    4
```

Circle **yes** or **no** to tell if you need to regroup 10 ones as 1 ten. Then add to find the sums.

1
```
  45      yes
 + 7
 _____     no
```
```
  34      yes
 + 3
 _____     no
```
```
  59      yes
 +23
 _____     no
```
```
  95      yes
 + 3
 _____     no
```

2
```
  39      yes
 +24
 _____     no
```
```
  17      yes
 +62
 _____     no
```
```
  75      yes
 + 9
 _____     no
```
```
  33      yes
 +28
 _____     no
```

3
```
  47      yes
 +40
 _____     no
```
```
  53      yes
 + 8
 _____     no
```
```
  46      yes
 +34
 _____     no
```
```
  47      yes
 +42
 _____     no
```

4
```
  15      yes
 + 5
 _____     no
```
```
  63      yes
 +27
 _____     no
```
```
  56      yes
 +25
 _____     no
```
```
  30      yes
 +19
 _____     no
```

5
```
  74      yes
 +19
 _____     no
```
```
  22      yes
 +71
 _____     no
```
```
  81      yes
 + 9
 _____     no
```
```
  19      yes
 +64
 _____     no
```

Addition—Regrouping

18

⭐ Add three numbers just as you would add two numbers together. Remember: Add the ones column first. If the answer is 10 or more, write the ones digit below the ones column. Write the tens above the tens column. Then add the tens column, including the tens you regrouped.

Add to find the sums. Regroup, if needed.

1

29	63	43	89	6	45
+ 9	+28	+32	+11	+37	+36

2

64	27	49	13	22	15
+26	+ 3	8	54	36	25
		+12	+ 7	+ 5	+30

3

70	28	37	16	34	36
18	42	35	23	91	18
+11	+ 4	+ 3	+20	+125	+41

4

48	15	64	44	38	79
+52	+84	+77	+37	+83	+10

5

14	12	44	12	34	49
47	68	23	37	32	12
+95	+17	+15	+43	+20	+30

Addition—Regrouping

19

⭐ When you add 3-digit numbers, you sometimes regroup 10 tens as 1 hundred.

Add the ones.	Add the tens.	Add the hundreds
$4 + 3 = 7$	$2 + 8 = 10$	$1 + 5 + 2 = 8$

hundreds	tens	ones
5	2	**4**
+ 2	8	**3**
		7

	hundreds	tens	ones
1	5	**2**	4
	+ 2	**8**	3
		0	7

	hundreds	tens	ones
1	**5**	2	4
	+ 2	8	3
	8	0	7

Add the digits in each place in the problem. Circle **ones**, **tens**, or **none** to show which place needs to be regrouped. Then add to solve.

1

257 +362	none tens ones	409 +390	none tens ones	89 +841	none tens ones	432 +338	none tens ones

2

509 +203	none tens ones	624 +194	none tens ones	213 +646	none tens ones	166 +343	none tens ones

3

350 +350	none tens ones	464 +327	none tens ones	621 +126	none tens ones	88 +220	none tens ones

Add to find the sum. Regroup ones or tens when needed.

4

219 +162	239 +143	138 +390	872 + 66	336 + 58	293 + 535

Name _____

20

Sometimes you will need to regroup more than once. Remember to add in your regrouped numbers!

	hundreds	tens	ones
	1	1	
	5	5	7
+	2	5	3
	8	1	0

Add. Regroup when needed.

1

254	426	638	372	845	543
+ 78	+334	+205	+263	+126	235
					+153

2

163	320	27	154	163	215
+ 89	+454	+538	321	327	432
			+503	+151	+ 54

3

290	256	342	563	457	223
324	309	122	304	340	215
+125	+ 70	+249	+ 26	+103	+175

4

231	114	858	328	413	524
+516	149	102	+348	137	+383
	+496	+ 32		+152	

5

128	370	872	141	159	806
39	+541	17	231	728	128
+125		+ 12	+102	+ 40	+ 74

Name _____

Take a Test Drive

Fill in the bubble beside the correct answer.

---

1   8
    +7

  ○ 13
  ○ 15
  ○ 56
  ○ 87

5   463
    + 35

  ○ 498
  ○ 508
  ○ 598
  ○ 813

---

2   45
    +32

  ○ 77
  ○ 87
  ○ 482
  ○ 4532

6   327
    +242

  ○ 569
  ○ 575
  ○ 579
  ○ 679

---

3   73
    +16

  ○ 79
  ○ 88
  ○ 89
  ○ 746

7 Bob picked 74 ears of corn. His brother worked longer and picked 213. How many ears of corn did they pick altogether?

  ○ 287
  ○ 289
  ○ 397
  ○ 953

---

4   359
    +120

  ○ 339
  ○ 479
  ○ 579
  ○ 589

8 For which problem would you need to regroup the ones place?

  ○   28   ○   54
     +31   +35

  ○   33   ○   63
     +27   +25

Advantage Math Grade 3 © 2004 Creative Teaching Press

Name _____

Take a Test Drive

Fill in the bubble beside the correct answer.

---

1 Which problem does not need to be regrouped?

$\bigcirc$ $\begin{array}{r} 28 \\ +53 \\ \hline \end{array}$ $\bigcirc$ $\begin{array}{r} 74 \\ + 9 \\ \hline \end{array}$

$\bigcirc$ $\begin{array}{r} 56 \\ +78 \\ \hline \end{array}$ $\bigcirc$ $\begin{array}{r} 46 \\ +32 \\ \hline \end{array}$

---

2 $\begin{array}{r} 29 \\ +31 \\ \hline \end{array}$

$\bigcirc$ 50
$\bigcirc$ 60
$\bigcirc$ 61
$\bigcirc$ 70

---

3 $\begin{array}{r} 87 \\ + 9 \\ \hline \end{array}$

$\bigcirc$ 86
$\bigcirc$ 92
$\bigcirc$ 96
$\bigcirc$ 879

---

4 Which problem does not need to be regrouped?

$\bigcirc$ $\begin{array}{r} 218 \\ +530 \\ \hline \end{array}$ $\bigcirc$ $\begin{array}{r} 307 \\ + 9 \\ \hline \end{array}$

$\bigcirc$ $\begin{array}{r} 562 \\ +178 \\ \hline \end{array}$ $\bigcirc$ $\begin{array}{r} 463 \\ +372 \\ \hline \end{array}$

---

5 $\begin{array}{r} 245 \\ +326 \\ \hline \end{array}$

$\bigcirc$ 561
$\bigcirc$ 571
$\bigcirc$ 661
$\bigcirc$ 671

---

6 $\begin{array}{r} 428 \\ +360 \\ \hline \end{array}$

$\bigcirc$ 788
$\bigcirc$ 798
$\bigcirc$ 888
$\bigcirc$ 898

---

7 By 8 p.m., there were 453 people in the theater. By the time the movie started 15 minutes later, 272 more had joined them. How many people were in the theater in all?

$\bigcirc$ 615
$\bigcirc$ 625
$\bigcirc$ 725
$\bigcirc$ 735

---

8 $\begin{array}{r} 53 \\ +678 \\ \hline \end{array}$

$\bigcirc$ 621
$\bigcirc$ 631
$\bigcirc$ 721
$\bigcirc$ 731

Subtraction—Mental Math

23

Subtract. Memorize these basic facts. Learn them by heart.

① $8 - 3 =$ _____ $14 - 5 =$ _____ $9 - 4 =$ _____ $12 - 4 =$ _____

② $16 - 7 =$ _____ $18 - 9 =$ _____ $10 - 2 =$ _____ $13 - 7 =$ _____

③ $12 - 9 =$ _____ $9 - 5 =$ _____ $15 - 7 =$ _____ $13 - 5 =$ _____

④
$$\begin{array}{r} 18 \\ -\ 9 \\ \hline \end{array} \qquad \begin{array}{r} 7 \\ -4 \\ \hline \end{array} \qquad \begin{array}{r} 15 \\ -\ 8 \\ \hline \end{array} \qquad \begin{array}{r} 12 \\ -\ 5 \\ \hline \end{array} \qquad \begin{array}{r} 20 \\ -10 \\ \hline \end{array} \qquad \begin{array}{r} 16 \\ -\ 8 \\ \hline \end{array}$$

⑤
$$\begin{array}{r} 13 \\ -\ 6 \\ \hline \end{array} \qquad \begin{array}{r} 9 \\ -5 \\ \hline \end{array} \qquad \begin{array}{r} 14 \\ -\ 8 \\ \hline \end{array} \qquad \begin{array}{r} 7 \\ -3 \\ \hline \end{array} \qquad \begin{array}{r} 12 \\ -\ 6 \\ \hline \end{array} \qquad \begin{array}{r} 8 \\ -4 \\ \hline \end{array}$$

⑥
$$\begin{array}{r} 17 \\ -17 \\ \hline \end{array} \qquad \begin{array}{r} 14 \\ -\ 7 \\ \hline \end{array} \qquad \begin{array}{r} 15 \\ -\ 9 \\ \hline \end{array} \qquad \begin{array}{r} 9 \\ -4 \\ \hline \end{array} \qquad \begin{array}{r} 12 \\ -\ 7 \\ \hline \end{array} \qquad \begin{array}{r} 15 \\ -\ 6 \\ \hline \end{array}$$

⑦
$$\begin{array}{r} 17 \\ -\ 8 \\ \hline \end{array} \qquad \begin{array}{r} 11 \\ -\ 4 \\ \hline \end{array} \qquad \begin{array}{r} 16 \\ -\ 9 \\ \hline \end{array} \qquad \begin{array}{r} 13 \\ -\ 8 \\ \hline \end{array} \qquad \begin{array}{r} 8 \\ -7 \\ \hline \end{array} \qquad \begin{array}{r} 11 \\ -\ 2 \\ \hline \end{array}$$

Subtraction—Mental Math

24

Subtract. Memorize these basic facts. Learn them by heart.

1) $10 - 6 =$ _____ $13 - 4 =$ _____ $11 - 5 =$ _____ $14 - 7 =$ _____

2) $16 - 8 =$ _____ $12 - 2 =$ _____ $15 - 6 =$ _____ $9 - 7 =$ _____

3) $13 - 9 =$ _____ $10 - 3 =$ _____ $8 - 5 =$ _____ $14 - 5 =$ _____

4)

$$\begin{array}{r} 11 \\ -\ 3 \\ \hline \end{array} \qquad \begin{array}{r} 14 \\ -\ 9 \\ \hline \end{array} \qquad \begin{array}{r} 7 \\ -7 \\ \hline \end{array} \qquad \begin{array}{r} 12 \\ -\ 8 \\ \hline \end{array} \qquad \begin{array}{r} 18 \\ -\ 9 \\ \hline \end{array} \qquad \begin{array}{r} 10 \\ -\ 6 \\ \hline \end{array}$$

5)

$$\begin{array}{r} 17 \\ -\ 8 \\ \hline \end{array} \qquad \begin{array}{r} 13 \\ -\ 5 \\ \hline \end{array} \qquad \begin{array}{r} 16 \\ -7 \\ \hline \end{array} \qquad \begin{array}{r} 8 \\ -7 \\ \hline \end{array} \qquad \begin{array}{r} 12 \\ -\ 4 \\ \hline \end{array} \qquad \begin{array}{r} 14 \\ -\ 6 \\ \hline \end{array}$$

6)

$$\begin{array}{r} 10 \\ -\ 8 \\ \hline \end{array} \qquad \begin{array}{r} 15 \\ -\ 6 \\ \hline \end{array} \qquad \begin{array}{r} 17 \\ -\ 9 \\ \hline \end{array} \qquad \begin{array}{r} 12 \\ -\ 5 \\ \hline \end{array} \qquad \begin{array}{r} 8 \\ -3 \\ \hline \end{array} \qquad \begin{array}{r} 9 \\ -2 \\ \hline \end{array}$$

7)

$$\begin{array}{r} 16 \\ -\ 8 \\ \hline \end{array} \qquad \begin{array}{r} 12 \\ -\ 6 \\ \hline \end{array} \qquad \begin{array}{r} 11 \\ -\ 5 \\ \hline \end{array} \qquad \begin{array}{r} 15 \\ -\ 8 \\ \hline \end{array} \qquad \begin{array}{r} 18 \\ -\ 9 \\ \hline \end{array} \qquad \begin{array}{r} 13 \\ -\ 6 \\ \hline \end{array}$$

Subtraction—No Regrouping

25

⭐ When you subtract, first subtract the digits in the ones place. Then subtract the digits in the tens place.

```
 tens ones
   5 6
 − 3 2
 ─────
     4
```

```
 tens ones
   5 6
 − 3 2
 ─────
   2 4
```

Solve.

1
| 37 | 24 | 39 | 46 | 57 | 95 |
| −17 | −12 | −28 | −13 | −23 | −42 |

2
| 82 | 39 | 49 | 35 | 49 | 73 |
| −20 | −17 | −26 | −23 | −30 | −21 |

3
| 45 | 56 | 68 | 67 | 92 | 79 |
| −23 | −35 | −31 | −32 | −21 | −32 |

4
| 86 | 40 | 77 | 49 | 93 | 78 |
| −23 | −30 | −46 | −19 | −22 | −25 |

5 Emily had 65 trading cards. She traded 23 cards that were doubles. How many cards did she keep? _____

6 Ryan's baseball team was to meet 48 times in the summer. By the middle of June, the team had met 16 times. How many more times would the team meet that summer?

_____

7 Juan's family drove 65 miles to visit a friend. On the way home, they stopped after 42 miles to rest. How many more miles did they have to drive to get home? _____

Name _____

26

⭐ When you find a difference, subtract the digits in the ones place first. Then subtract the digits in the tens place. Finally, subtract the digits in the hundreds place.

hundreds tens ones	hundreds tens ones	hundreds tens ones
265	265	265
−140	−140	−140
5	25	125

Solve.

1

488	365	494	687	397	552
− 17	−342	−172	− 43	−166	−411

2

162	237	588	745	214	830
−141	−122	−356	−324	−110	−710

3

935	769	478	523	284	505
−524	−602	− 25	−423	−173	−201

4

495	851	168	344	827	716
−334	− 50	− 18	−342	−406	−513

5 There were 272 students in the third grade. 31 moved away during the summer. How many third-grade students were left to start school in the fall? _____

6 The grocery store had 145 apples for sale on Thursday. Shoppers bought 123 apples that day. How many apples were left in the store? _____

7 Patrick had 330 letters to deliver on his mail route. By noon he had delivered 220 letters. How many letters did he have left to deliver? _____

Name _____

27

★ When subtracting, look at the ones column first. If the bottom digit is greater than the top digit, you need to regroup.

```
 tens ones
  2  11
   3 1
 -1 8
 ――――
     3
```

Look at the ones column. Since 8 is greater than 1, you need to regroup. Take 1 ten from the tens place. Add it to the ones. Subtract the ones. Then subtract the tens.

```
 tens ones
  2  11
   3 1
 -1 8
 ――――
   1 3
```

Circle **yes** or **no** to tell if you need to regroup. Then subtract to solve.

1
```
 43      yes        28      yes        43      yes        57      yes
- 8                -16                -15                -28
        no                 no                 no                 no
```

2
```
 80      yes        52      yes        71      yes        63      yes
-57                -12                -29                -44
        no                 no                 no                 no
```

3
```
 32      yes        87      yes        35      yes        46      yes
-23                -48                -27                -18
        no                 no                 no                 no
```

4
```
 23      yes        30      yes        51      yes        72      yes
- 5                -22                -15                -33
        no                 no                 no                 no
```

5
```
 46      yes        60      yes        56      yes        32      yes
-37                -26                -37                - 8
        no                 no                 no                 no
```

Subtraction—Regrouping

28

⭐ Remember to regroup when the digit in the bottom number is greater than the digit in the top number.

$$\begin{array}{r} \overset{\text{tens ones}}{\overset{4 \;\; 15}{\cancel{5}\cancel{5}}} \\ -2\,6 \\ \hline 2\,9 \end{array}$$

Subtract. Regroup when needed.

1
$\begin{array}{r} 43 \\ -17 \\ \hline \end{array}$
$\begin{array}{r} 67 \\ -\;9 \\ \hline \end{array}$
$\begin{array}{r} 94 \\ -23 \\ \hline \end{array}$
$\begin{array}{r} 85 \\ -37 \\ \hline \end{array}$
$\begin{array}{r} 25 \\ -14 \\ \hline \end{array}$
$\begin{array}{r} 70 \\ -36 \\ \hline \end{array}$

2
$\begin{array}{r} 93 \\ -15 \\ \hline \end{array}$
$\begin{array}{r} 56 \\ -27 \\ \hline \end{array}$
$\begin{array}{r} 86 \\ -36 \\ \hline \end{array}$
$\begin{array}{r} 61 \\ -38 \\ \hline \end{array}$
$\begin{array}{r} 47 \\ -\;9 \\ \hline \end{array}$
$\begin{array}{r} 76 \\ -58 \\ \hline \end{array}$

3
$\begin{array}{r} 48 \\ -29 \\ \hline \end{array}$
$\begin{array}{r} 54 \\ -46 \\ \hline \end{array}$
$\begin{array}{r} 72 \\ -16 \\ \hline \end{array}$
$\begin{array}{r} 55 \\ -33 \\ \hline \end{array}$
$\begin{array}{r} 60 \\ -34 \\ \hline \end{array}$
$\begin{array}{r} 87 \\ -\;9 \\ \hline \end{array}$

4
$\begin{array}{r} 42 \\ -17 \\ \hline \end{array}$
$\begin{array}{r} 53 \\ -34 \\ \hline \end{array}$
$\begin{array}{r} 26 \\ -\;8 \\ \hline \end{array}$
$\begin{array}{r} 35 \\ -19 \\ \hline \end{array}$
$\begin{array}{r} 81 \\ -46 \\ \hline \end{array}$
$\begin{array}{r} 77 \\ -58 \\ \hline \end{array}$

5
$\begin{array}{r} 92 \\ -44 \\ \hline \end{array}$
$\begin{array}{r} 72 \\ -33 \\ \hline \end{array}$
$\begin{array}{r} 37 \\ -28 \\ \hline \end{array}$
$\begin{array}{r} 80 \\ -68 \\ \hline \end{array}$
$\begin{array}{r} 27 \\ -19 \\ \hline \end{array}$
$\begin{array}{r} 91 \\ -67 \\ \hline \end{array}$

Subtraction—Regrouping

29

⭐ When the tens digit in the number you are subtracting is greater than the tens digit in the number you are subtracting from, regroup from the hundreds place.

```
      hundreds  tens  ones
         2   15
         3̶   5̶    8
      -  2   8    4
      _____
             7    4
```

Look at the tens column. Since 8 is greater than 5, you need to regroup. Take 1 hundred from the hundreds place. Add it to the tens.

Subtract. Regroup when needed.

1
```
 437      634      374      872      724      464
-163     -217     -204     -342     -518     -272
```

2
```
 934      208      537      542      683      492
-480     - 84     -229     -281     -580     -365
```

3
```
 509      768      838      356      288      655
-162     -159     -472     -258     -198     -292
```

4
```
 716      574      981      877      366      227
-307     -482     -804     -182     -291     -119
```

5 The Student Council had 500 tickets for the band concert. They sold 250 tickets. How many tickets were left unsold? _____

6 There were 361 people at the pool. 256 went home after it started to rain. How many people were left? _____

Subtraction—Regrouping

30

⭐ Sometimes you will need to regroup more than once.

```
      hundreds tens ones
         4  12  13
         5̶  3̶  3̶
      -  3  4  4
      ─────────
         1  8  9
```

Subtract. Regroup when needed.

1
542	327	840	245	437	508
-143	- 96	-243	-156	-229	-126

2
624	953	729	286	448	263
-315	-624	-693	-107	-359	-175

3
457	764	921	685	818	550
-366	-686	-755	-492	-567	-362

4
270	992	713	454	882	677
-125	-547	-681	-178	-634	-508

5
591	916	530	369	431	212
-349	-444	-276	- 82	-185	-179

Check with Inverse Operations

31

⭐ Subtraction and addition are opposites. Use one to check the other.

When you add:
$$\begin{array}{r} 13 \\ +24 \\ \hline 37 \end{array}$$

Check with subtraction:
$$\begin{array}{r} 37 \\ -24 \\ \hline 13 \end{array}$$

When you subtract:
$$\begin{array}{r} 58 \\ -29 \\ \hline 29 \end{array}$$

Check with addition:
$$\begin{array}{r} 29 \\ +29 \\ \hline 58 \end{array}$$

Use the inverse operation to check each equation. Circle the equations that are correct. Cross out equations that are incorrect.

1

$$\begin{array}{r} 58 \\ -21 \\ \hline 37 \end{array} \quad \begin{array}{r} 37 \\ +21 \\ \hline 58 \end{array} \qquad \begin{array}{r} 35 \\ +26 \\ \hline 61 \end{array} \qquad \begin{array}{r} 53 \\ +34 \\ \hline 81 \end{array} \qquad \begin{array}{r} 48 \\ -34 \\ \hline 4 \end{array}$$

2

$$\begin{array}{r} 35 \\ +48 \\ \hline 83 \end{array} \qquad \begin{array}{r} 53 \\ -47 \\ \hline 6 \end{array} \qquad \begin{array}{r} 62 \\ +17 \\ \hline 79 \end{array} \qquad \begin{array}{r} 54 \\ -22 \\ \hline 32 \end{array}$$

3

$$\begin{array}{r} 76 \\ +19 \\ \hline 67 \end{array} \qquad \begin{array}{r} 81 \\ -12 \\ \hline 78 \end{array} \qquad \begin{array}{r} 60 \\ +39 \\ \hline 89 \end{array} \qquad \begin{array}{r} 38 \\ -29 \\ \hline 9 \end{array}$$

4

$$\begin{array}{r} 11 \\ +45 \\ \hline 56 \end{array} \qquad \begin{array}{r} 60 \\ -47 \\ \hline 23 \end{array} \qquad \begin{array}{r} 42 \\ +36 \\ \hline 98 \end{array} \qquad \begin{array}{r} 85 \\ -9 \\ \hline 76 \end{array}$$

5

$$\begin{array}{r} 25 \\ +29 \\ \hline 44 \end{array} \qquad \begin{array}{r} 47 \\ -18 \\ \hline 29 \end{array} \qquad \begin{array}{r} 66 \\ +27 \\ \hline 93 \end{array} \qquad \begin{array}{r} 73 \\ -44 \\ \hline 39 \end{array}$$

Name _____

Check with Inverse Operations

32

Use the inverse operation to check each equation. Circle the equations that are correct. Cross out equations that are incorrect.

①
$$\begin{array}{r} 329 \\ -118 \\ \hline 111 \end{array} \quad \begin{array}{r} 118 \\ +111 \\ \hline 229 \end{array} \qquad \begin{array}{r} 247 \\ +429 \\ \hline 766 \end{array} \qquad \begin{array}{r} 523 \\ +238 \\ \hline 761 \end{array} \qquad \begin{array}{r} 805 \\ -323 \\ \hline 582 \end{array}$$

②
$$\begin{array}{r} 297 \\ +382 \\ \hline 689 \end{array} \qquad \begin{array}{r} 485 \\ - 96 \\ \hline 389 \end{array} \qquad \begin{array}{r} 653 \\ +291 \\ \hline 944 \end{array} \qquad \begin{array}{r} 556 \\ -387 \\ \hline 269 \end{array}$$

③
$$\begin{array}{r} 249 \\ +650 \\ \hline 899 \end{array} \qquad \begin{array}{r} 736 \\ -186 \\ \hline 650 \end{array} \qquad \begin{array}{r} 345 \\ +396 \\ \hline 741 \end{array} \qquad \begin{array}{r} 278 \\ -109 \\ \hline 169 \end{array}$$

④
$$\begin{array}{r} 714 \\ +255 \\ \hline 979 \end{array} \qquad \begin{array}{r} 637 \\ -568 \\ \hline 69 \end{array} \qquad \begin{array}{r} 180 \\ +247 \\ \hline 317 \end{array} \qquad \begin{array}{r} 454 \\ -318 \\ \hline 136 \end{array}$$

⑤ Kyle read a book with 263 pages. Lisa read a book with 255 pages. How many pages did Kyle and Lisa read altogether? _____

⑥ Maggie's family must drive 427 miles to visit her grandparents. Her family has already driven 336 miles. How many miles are left to drive? _____

⑦ 530 people came to cheer on the local baseball team. 148 people came from another town to cheer on the other team. How many people came to the game altogether? _____

Take a Test Drive

Fill in the bubble beside the correct answer.

1
$$\begin{array}{r} 48 \\ -27 \\ \hline \end{array}$$

○ 11
○ 21
○ 35
○ 75

---

5 Which needs to be regrouped?

○ $\begin{array}{r} 35 \\ -24 \\ \hline \end{array}$ ○ $\begin{array}{r} 97 \\ -95 \\ \hline \end{array}$

○ $\begin{array}{r} 46 \\ -25 \\ \hline \end{array}$ ○ $\begin{array}{r} 53 \\ -28 \\ \hline \end{array}$

2
$$\begin{array}{r} 64 \\ -30 \\ \hline \end{array}$$

○ 24
○ 30
○ 34
○ 94

---

6 Which needs to be regrouped?

○ $\begin{array}{r} 139 \\ -29 \\ \hline \end{array}$ ○ $\begin{array}{r} 348 \\ -257 \\ \hline \end{array}$

○ $\begin{array}{r} 723 \\ -603 \\ \hline \end{array}$ ○ $\begin{array}{r} 462 \\ -341 \\ \hline \end{array}$

3
$$\begin{array}{r} 365 \\ -245 \\ \hline \end{array}$$

○ 22
○ 112
○ 120
○ 612

---

7 Brandon's mom helped him cut his birthday cake into 24 pieces. His family ate 9 pieces. How many pieces were left?

○ 21
○ 15
○ 33
○ 12

4
$$\begin{array}{r} 598 \\ -395 \\ \hline \end{array}$$

○ 103
○ 183
○ 203
○ 993

---

8 Hannah's pet fish had 45 babies! Hannah gave away 33. How many baby fish did she keep?

○ 78
○ 45
○ 12
○ 22

Take a Test Drive

Fill in the bubble beside the correct answer.

1

32
−28

○ 4
○ 14
○ 50
○ 60

2

83
−45

○ 32
○ 38
○ 42
○ 47

3 There are 672 students in Pace Elementary. Today, 118 of these students are home sick. How many students came to school today?

○ 554
○ 403
○ 117
○ 599

4 Kevin brought 386 oranges to sell at the market. Susan brought 259 oranges to sell. How many oranges did they bring altogether?

○ 127
○ 412
○ 645
○ 982

5

543
−244

○ 201
○ 299
○ 301
○ 399

6

635
− 58

○ 577
○ 587
○ 683
○ 693

7 Which would you use to check this equation?
84 − 36 = 48

○ 84 + 36 = ?
○ 36 − 84 = ?
○ 36 + 48 = ?
○ 42 + 42 = ?

8 Use inverse operations to find which equation is incorrect.

○ 97 − 49 = 48
○ 85 − 60 = 25
○ 53 − 37 = 16
○ 72 − 44 = 32

Name _____

Skip Counting

35

⭐ When you skip count, you skip certain numbers and count by 2's or 3's or 4's and so on. If you are not certain what the next number is, add the number you are counting by to the previous number.

Counting by 4: 4, 8, 12, 16, 20, 24, 28, 32, 36, 40...
|
12 + 4 = 16

Follow the pattern to continue skip counting by the number given.

1 **by 2:** 2, 4, 6, _8_ _____

2 **by 5:** 5, 10, 15, _____

3 **by 10:** 10, 20, 30, _____

4 **by 3:** 3, 6, 9, _____

5 **by 6:** 6, 12, 18, _____

Look at the patterns. Draw a line to match the skip counting pattern with the number.

by 2:	3, 6, 9, 12, 15, 18
by 3:	4, 8, 12, 16, 20, 24
by 4:	5, 10, 15, 20, 25, 30
by 5:	2, 4, 6, 8, 10, 12
by 6:	10, 20, 30, 40, 50, 60
by 10:	6, 12, 18, 24, 30, 36

Skip Counting

36

⭐ Each time you skip count, you make a pattern of numbers. When you skip count by 2, you add 2 to a number to find the next number.

Skip count by the number given. Write the first 6 numbers in the pattern.

1 by 7: __7__, __14__, _____, _____, _____, _____, _____

2 by 8: _____, _____, _____, _____, _____, _____, _____

3 by 9: _____, _____, _____, _____, _____, _____, _____

4 by 20: _____, _____, _____, _____, _____, _____, _____

5 by 25: _____, _____, _____, _____, _____, _____, _____

6 by 100: _____, _____, _____, _____, _____, _____, _____

7 Look at item 2 above. What will be the 8th number in the pattern? _____

8 What will be the 11th number? _____

9 Look at item 4 above. What will be the 9th number in the pattern? _____

10 What will be the 10th number? _____

11 Look at item 6 above. What will be the 10th number in the pattern? _____

12 What will be the 20th number? _____

Multiplication

37

⭐ 3 x 2 is read "three times two."

3 x 2 = ☆☆ ☆☆ ☆☆
        2 + 2 + 2

Solve.

1
$\begin{array}{r} 4 \\ \times 6 \\ \hline \end{array}$
$\begin{array}{r} 1 \\ \times 8 \\ \hline \end{array}$
$\begin{array}{r} 7 \\ \times 2 \\ \hline \end{array}$
$\begin{array}{r} 9 \\ \times 6 \\ \hline \end{array}$
$\begin{array}{r} 4 \\ \times 9 \\ \hline \end{array}$
$\begin{array}{r} 5 \\ \times 7 \\ \hline \end{array}$

2
$\begin{array}{r} 8 \\ \times 4 \\ \hline \end{array}$
$\begin{array}{r} 7 \\ \times 1 \\ \hline \end{array}$
$\begin{array}{r} 2 \\ \times 2 \\ \hline \end{array}$
$\begin{array}{r} 4 \\ \times 3 \\ \hline \end{array}$
$\begin{array}{r} 3 \\ \times 5 \\ \hline \end{array}$
$\begin{array}{r} 8 \\ \times 5 \\ \hline \end{array}$

3
$\begin{array}{r} 7 \\ \times 6 \\ \hline \end{array}$
$\begin{array}{r} 6 \\ \times 2 \\ \hline \end{array}$
$\begin{array}{r} 9 \\ \times 8 \\ \hline \end{array}$
$\begin{array}{r} 6 \\ \times 6 \\ \hline \end{array}$
$\begin{array}{r} 5 \\ \times 9 \\ \hline \end{array}$
$\begin{array}{r} 4 \\ \times 2 \\ \hline \end{array}$

4
$\begin{array}{r} 2 \\ \times 5 \\ \hline \end{array}$
$\begin{array}{r} 7 \\ \times 7 \\ \hline \end{array}$
$\begin{array}{r} 5 \\ \times 6 \\ \hline \end{array}$
$\begin{array}{r} 1 \\ \times 3 \\ \hline \end{array}$
$\begin{array}{r} 2 \\ \times 7 \\ \hline \end{array}$
$\begin{array}{r} 7 \\ \times 8 \\ \hline \end{array}$

5
$\begin{array}{r} 1 \\ \times 9 \\ \hline \end{array}$
$\begin{array}{r} 5 \\ \times 6 \\ \hline \end{array}$
$\begin{array}{r} 2 \\ \times 4 \\ \hline \end{array}$
$\begin{array}{r} 4 \\ \times 4 \\ \hline \end{array}$
$\begin{array}{r} 8 \\ \times 3 \\ \hline \end{array}$
$\begin{array}{r} 8 \\ \times 6 \\ \hline \end{array}$

6 The playground has 4 swing sets. There are 4 swings in each set. How many swings are there in all? _____

7 Eric and Cori sold lemonade for 2 days. They sold 9 cups of lemonade each day. How many cups did they sell altogether? _____

Multiplication

38

Solve the following problems.

1

6	3	5	9	3	7
×4	×9	×7	×9	×4	×3

2

8	5	2	6	2	8
×8	×5	×8	×3	×2	×4

3

8	9	1	6	4	6
×6	×6	×5	×6	×8	×7

4

2	9	7	5	3	7
×5	×8	×7	×4	×2	×4

5

1	9	7	2	3	5
×3	×3	×6	×1	×3	×9

6 Shanta is planning a picnic for her and 6 friends. She wants each person to get 3 cookies. How many cookies does Shanta need to buy? _____

7 Vivek has a garden with 5 sections. He has planted 8 plants in each section. How many plants is Vivek growing? _____

8 Brookville Elementary had a basketball tournament. 9 teams played in the tournament. There were 3 coaches for each team. How many coaches were at the tournament? _____

Multiplication

39

⭐ When you multiply by 0, the product is 0. 3 x 0 = 0
When you multiply by 1, the product is the other factor. 3 x 1 = 3

Solve.

1
$$15 \times 2$$ $$11 \times 0$$ $$4 \times 1$$ $$7 \times 10$$ $$6 \times 0$$ $$2 \times 5$$

2
$$8 \times 8$$ $$8 \times 1$$ $$3 \times 2$$ $$10 \times 2$$ $$5 \times 1$$ $$18 \times 0$$

3
$$6 \times 10$$ $$9 \times 2$$ $$2 \times 2$$ $$13 \times 1$$ $$17 \times 0$$ $$15 \times 1$$

4
$$11 \times 2$$ $$14 \times 0$$ $$6 \times 1$$ $$8 \times 2$$ $$5 \times 10$$ $$2 \times 0$$

5
$$16 \times 1$$ $$7 \times 2$$ $$9 \times 10$$ $$3 \times 0$$ $$20 \times 1$$ $$12 \times 1$$

6 Nonnie has 2 vases. There are 6 flowers in each vase. How many flowers does Nonnie have in all? _____

7 7 pencils come in a pack. Anna has 1 pack of pencils. How many pencils does Anna have? _____

Name _____

Multiplication

40

⭐ When you multiply a double-digit number with a single-digit number, multiply the digits in the ones place first. Then multiply the digit in the tens place with the single-digit number.

$$\begin{array}{r} 52 \\ \times 4 \\ \hline 8 \end{array} \qquad \begin{array}{r} 52 \\ \times 4 \\ \hline 208 \end{array}$$

Solve.

1
$$\begin{array}{r} 12 \\ \times 3 \\ \hline \end{array} \qquad \begin{array}{r} 64 \\ \times 2 \\ \hline \end{array} \qquad \begin{array}{r} 70 \\ \times 7 \\ \hline \end{array} \qquad \begin{array}{r} 8 \\ \times 6 \\ \hline \end{array} \qquad \begin{array}{r} 57 \\ \times 1 \\ \hline \end{array} \qquad \begin{array}{r} 40 \\ \times 8 \\ \hline \end{array}$$

2
$$\begin{array}{r} 24 \\ \times 2 \\ \hline \end{array} \qquad \begin{array}{r} 30 \\ \times 9 \\ \hline \end{array} \qquad \begin{array}{r} 7 \\ \times 5 \\ \hline \end{array} \qquad \begin{array}{r} 80 \\ \times 6 \\ \hline \end{array} \qquad \begin{array}{r} 10 \\ \times 6 \\ \hline \end{array} \qquad \begin{array}{r} 42 \\ \times 3 \\ \hline \end{array}$$

3
$$\begin{array}{r} 7 \\ \times 6 \\ \hline \end{array} \qquad \begin{array}{r} 25 \\ \times 1 \\ \hline \end{array} \qquad \begin{array}{r} 51 \\ \times 5 \\ \hline \end{array} \qquad \begin{array}{r} 50 \\ \times 4 \\ \hline \end{array} \qquad \begin{array}{r} 36 \\ \times 1 \\ \hline \end{array} \qquad \begin{array}{r} 70 \\ \times 3 \\ \hline \end{array}$$

4
$$\begin{array}{r} 20 \\ \times 6 \\ \hline \end{array} \qquad \begin{array}{r} 11 \\ \times 5 \\ \hline \end{array} \qquad \begin{array}{r} 60 \\ \times 7 \\ \hline \end{array} \qquad \begin{array}{r} 9 \\ \times 9 \\ \hline \end{array} \qquad \begin{array}{r} 42 \\ \times 4 \\ \hline \end{array} \qquad \begin{array}{r} 32 \\ \times 3 \\ \hline \end{array}$$

5
$$\begin{array}{r} 10 \\ \times 5 \\ \hline \end{array} \qquad \begin{array}{r} 54 \\ \times 2 \\ \hline \end{array} \qquad \begin{array}{r} 70 \\ \times 8 \\ \hline \end{array} \qquad \begin{array}{r} 66 \\ \times 1 \\ \hline \end{array} \qquad \begin{array}{r} 30 \\ \times 6 \\ \hline \end{array} \qquad \begin{array}{r} 20 \\ \times 2 \\ \hline \end{array}$$

6 There are 21 houses on Maple Drive. 5 people live in each house. How many people live on Maple Drive? _____

7 There are 30 classrooms at Valley Elementary School. Each room has 4 chalkboards. How many chalkboards are there at Valley Elementary School? _____

Multiplication

41

Solve the following problems.

1.
$$\begin{array}{r} 10 \\ \times\ 7 \\ \hline \end{array}$$
$$\begin{array}{r} 53 \\ \times\ 3 \\ \hline \end{array}$$
$$\begin{array}{r} 81 \\ \times\ 5 \\ \hline \end{array}$$
$$\begin{array}{r} 41 \\ \times\ 3 \\ \hline \end{array}$$
$$\begin{array}{r} 20 \\ \times\ 8 \\ \hline \end{array}$$
$$\begin{array}{r} 91 \\ \times\ 6 \\ \hline \end{array}$$

2.
$$\begin{array}{r} 82 \\ \times\ 3 \\ \hline \end{array}$$
$$\begin{array}{r} 10 \\ \times\ 6 \\ \hline \end{array}$$
$$\begin{array}{r} 72 \\ \times\ 4 \\ \hline \end{array}$$
$$\begin{array}{r} 8 \\ \times 7 \\ \hline \end{array}$$
$$\begin{array}{r} 50 \\ \times\ 8 \\ \hline \end{array}$$
$$\begin{array}{r} 44 \\ \times\ 2 \\ \hline \end{array}$$

3.
$$\begin{array}{r} 18 \\ \times\ 2 \\ \hline \end{array}$$
$$\begin{array}{r} 20 \\ \times\ 5 \\ \hline \end{array}$$
$$\begin{array}{r} 37 \\ \times\ 2 \\ \hline \end{array}$$
$$\begin{array}{r} 92 \\ \times\ 4 \\ \hline \end{array}$$
$$\begin{array}{r} 61 \\ \times\ 4 \\ \hline \end{array}$$
$$\begin{array}{r} 51 \\ \times\ 2 \\ \hline \end{array}$$

4.
$$\begin{array}{r} 11 \\ \times\ 4 \\ \hline \end{array}$$
$$\begin{array}{r} 70 \\ \times\ 7 \\ \hline \end{array}$$
$$\begin{array}{r} 23 \\ \times\ 3 \\ \hline \end{array}$$
$$\begin{array}{r} 40 \\ \times\ 7 \\ \hline \end{array}$$
$$\begin{array}{r} 6 \\ \times 4 \\ \hline \end{array}$$
$$\begin{array}{r} 24 \\ \times\ 3 \\ \hline \end{array}$$

5.
$$\begin{array}{r} 59 \\ \times\ 1 \\ \hline \end{array}$$
$$\begin{array}{r} 91 \\ \times\ 3 \\ \hline \end{array}$$
$$\begin{array}{r} 60 \\ \times\ 7 \\ \hline \end{array}$$
$$\begin{array}{r} 34 \\ \times\ 2 \\ \hline \end{array}$$
$$\begin{array}{r} 47 \\ \times\ 1 \\ \hline \end{array}$$
$$\begin{array}{r} 20 \\ \times\ 9 \\ \hline \end{array}$$

6. Nathan carried 2 bags home from the grocery store. Each bag weighed 13 pounds. How many pounds did Nathan carry? _____

7. There are 50 graham crackers in a box. Gayle bought 4 boxes. How many graham crackers did she buy? _____

8. There are 70 pages in a workbook. There are 8 workbooks in a package. How many pages are in one package? _____

Multiplication

42

Solve the following problems.

1.
23	27	36	25	28	38
× 2	× 4	× 2	× 3	× 2	× 3

2.
21	17	12	16	25	13
× 4	× 6	× 9	× 5	× 4	× 6

3.
18	49	37	26	36	33
× 2	× 2	× 2	× 2	× 3	× 2

4.
19	12	14	40	15	24
× 3	× 8	× 6	× 7	× 5	× 3

5.
18	17	27	18	16	12
× 6	× 4	× 2	× 9	× 7	× 6

6. Kelly and Dawn each have 19 colored pencils. How many colored pencils do they have altogether? _____

7. 12 peaches come in a bag. Bryce buys 7 bags of peaches. How many peaches does he have? _____

8. There are 15 more weeks of school. If there are 5 school days in one week, how many days of school are left? _____

Multiplication

43

Solve the following problems.

1.
$$\begin{array}{r} 18 \\ \times\,4 \\ \hline \end{array}$$
$$\begin{array}{r} 38 \\ \times\,2 \\ \hline \end{array}$$
$$\begin{array}{r} 27 \\ \times\,3 \\ \hline \end{array}$$
$$\begin{array}{r} 13 \\ \times\,7 \\ \hline \end{array}$$
$$\begin{array}{r} 14 \\ \times\,8 \\ \hline \end{array}$$
$$\begin{array}{r} 19 \\ \times\,5 \\ \hline \end{array}$$

2.
$$\begin{array}{r} 16 \\ \times\,8 \\ \hline \end{array}$$
$$\begin{array}{r} 25 \\ \times\,2 \\ \hline \end{array}$$
$$\begin{array}{r} 38 \\ \times\,3 \\ \hline \end{array}$$
$$\begin{array}{r} 13 \\ \times\,9 \\ \hline \end{array}$$
$$\begin{array}{r} 12 \\ \times\,6 \\ \hline \end{array}$$
$$\begin{array}{r} 26 \\ \times\,3 \\ \hline \end{array}$$

3.
$$\begin{array}{r} 29 \\ \times\,2 \\ \hline \end{array}$$
$$\begin{array}{r} 37 \\ \times\,2 \\ \hline \end{array}$$
$$\begin{array}{r} 46 \\ \times\,2 \\ \hline \end{array}$$
$$\begin{array}{r} 16 \\ \times\,3 \\ \hline \end{array}$$
$$\begin{array}{r} 14 \\ \times\,5 \\ \hline \end{array}$$
$$\begin{array}{r} 12 \\ \times\,5 \\ \hline \end{array}$$

4.
$$\begin{array}{r} 24 \\ \times\,4 \\ \hline \end{array}$$
$$\begin{array}{r} 16 \\ \times\,6 \\ \hline \end{array}$$
$$\begin{array}{r} 23 \\ \times\,4 \\ \hline \end{array}$$
$$\begin{array}{r} 17 \\ \times\,5 \\ \hline \end{array}$$
$$\begin{array}{r} 15 \\ \times\,9 \\ \hline \end{array}$$
$$\begin{array}{r} 24 \\ \times\,3 \\ \hline \end{array}$$

5.
$$\begin{array}{r} 47 \\ \times\,2 \\ \hline \end{array}$$
$$\begin{array}{r} 12 \\ \times\,9 \\ \hline \end{array}$$
$$\begin{array}{r} 28 \\ \times\,3 \\ \hline \end{array}$$
$$\begin{array}{r} 19 \\ \times\,4 \\ \hline \end{array}$$
$$\begin{array}{r} 45 \\ \times\,2 \\ \hline \end{array}$$
$$\begin{array}{r} 18 \\ \times\,3 \\ \hline \end{array}$$

6. Hugh ate 12 cherries each day for 7 days in a row. How many cherries did Hugh eat? _____

7. There are 29 T-shirts on a rack. There are 4 racks in the store. How many T-shirts are there in the store? _____

8. There are 13 stairs in a staircase. The apartment complex has 5 staircases. How many stairs are there in the complex? _____

Division

44

⭐ ÷ and ⟌ ‾‾‾ mean divide. You can use division to find how many items are in a group or to find out how many groups there are.

There are 6 ♡'s. There are 3 ♡'s in each group. How many groups are there? 6 ÷ 3 = **2**

There are 6 ♡'s. There are 2 groups. How many are there in each group? 6 ÷ 2 = **3**

Solve.

1 $45 \div 5 =$ $9 \div 3 =$ $2 \div 1 =$ $42 \div 6 =$ $12 \div 3 =$ $28 \div 7 =$

2 $6 \div 2 =$ $72 \div 8 =$ $49 \div 7 =$ $10 \div 5 =$ $42 \div 7 =$ $32 \div 4 =$

3 $36 \div 6 =$ $5 \div 1 =$ $54 \div 6 =$ $18 \div 3 =$ $16 \div 8 =$ $25 \div 5 =$

4 $64 \div 8 =$ $21 \div 7 =$ $12 \div 4 =$ $81 \div 9 =$ $35 \div 5 =$ $27 \div 3 =$

5 $24 \div 6 =$ $48 \div 6 =$ $16 \div 4 =$ $8 \div 2 =$ $30 \div 6 =$ $9 \div 1 =$

6 Aisha's class needs parents to drive them to the bowling alley. There are 28 people in Aisha's class. There are 4 passenger seats in each car. How many cars do they need? _____

7 Devin has 42 photos. He wants to put them in an album. Each album page can hold 6 photos. How many pages will Devin use? _____

Division

45

Solve the following problems.

1. $30 \div 5 =$ $36 \div 9 =$ $9 \div 3 =$ $45 \div 5 =$ $72 \div 8 =$ $12 \div 2 =$

2. $4 \div 2 =$ $9 \div 1 =$ $14 \div 2 =$ $54 \div 6 =$ $18 \div 2 =$ $20 \div 5 =$

3. $6 \div 6 =$ $18 \div 3 =$ $10 \div 2 =$ $48 \div 8 =$ $16 \div 8 =$ $63 \div 9 =$

4. $49 \div 7 =$ $36 \div 6 =$ $28 \div 7 =$ $25 \div 5 =$ $64 \div 8 =$ $2 \div 2 =$

5. $7 \div 1 =$ $15 \div 3 =$ $81 \div 9 =$ $42 \div 7 =$ $40 \div 8 =$ $12 \div 4 =$

6. Mr. Samuel and Ms. Luce have 48 students in their combined classes. They want to divide the students into groups of 6. How many students will be in each group? _____

7. There are 56 trees and 7 houses on Blackberry Lane. If each house has the same number of trees, how many trees are in each yard? _____

8. Every week Jonah gets $5 when he completes his chores. Jonah is saving this money to buy a soccer ball that costs $40. How many weeks will it take before he has enough money for the soccer ball? _____

Division

46

Solve the following problems.

1 $1\overline{)13}$ $1\overline{)15}$ $10\overline{)90}$ $5\overline{)35}$ $1\overline{)19}$ $10\overline{)60}$

2 $1\overline{)4}$ $5\overline{)25}$ $5\overline{)15}$ $10\overline{)70}$ $1\overline{)8}$ $5\overline{)30}$

3 $10\overline{)80}$ $10\overline{)20}$ $1\overline{)10}$ $1\overline{)5}$ $10\overline{)40}$ $5\overline{)5}$

4 $10\overline{)30}$ $1\overline{)14}$ $5\overline{)45}$ $5\overline{)10}$ $10\overline{)10}$ $1\overline{)6}$

5 $5\overline{)40}$ $1\overline{)18}$ $1\overline{)20}$ $1\overline{)16}$ $5\overline{)20}$ $1\overline{)17}$

6 30 markers come in a pack. How many markers will each of 5 children get if the markers are split evenly among them? _____

7 There are 60 balloons at the booth. There are 10 children who want balloons. How many balloons will each child get if the balloons are split evenly among them? _____

8 A pizza comes cut into 15 slices. There are 5 people in the Chaker family. How many slices does each person get if each gets the same number of slices? _____

Advantage Math Grade 3 © 2004 Creative Teaching Press

Fact Families

47

Solve the following problems.

1. $\begin{array}{r} 6 \\ \times 4 \\ \hline \end{array}$ $6\overline{)24}$ $\begin{array}{r} 4 \\ \times 6 \\ \hline \end{array}$ $4\overline{)24}$

2. $\begin{array}{r} 7 \\ \times 5 \\ \hline \end{array}$ $7\overline{)35}$ $\begin{array}{r} 5 \\ \times 7 \\ \hline \end{array}$ $5\overline{)35}$

3. $\begin{array}{r} 9 \\ \times 8 \\ \hline \end{array}$ $9\overline{)72}$ $\begin{array}{r} 8 \\ \times 9 \\ \hline \end{array}$ $8\overline{)72}$

4. $\begin{array}{r} 3 \\ \times 5 \\ \hline \end{array}$ $5\overline{)15}$ $\begin{array}{r} 5 \\ \times 3 \\ \hline \end{array}$ $3\overline{)15}$

5. $\begin{array}{r} 2 \\ \times 8 \\ \hline \end{array}$ $2\overline{)16}$ $\begin{array}{r} 8 \\ \times 2 \\ \hline \end{array}$ $8\overline{)16}$

6. Each chapter in LaShaun's book has 8 pages. There are 7 chapters in the book. How many pages does the book have? _____

7. Farrah has 3 friends. The 4 girls each know 3 different card tricks. How many card tricks do they know altogether? _____

8. There are 5 kids in the Connell family. Each kid will eat 6 strawberries after dinner. How many strawberries does Mrs. Connell need to buy? _____

Fact Families

48

Solve the following problems.

1. $6\overline{)48}$ $\begin{array}{r} 6 \\ \times 8 \\ \hline \end{array}$ $8\overline{)48}$ $\begin{array}{r} 8 \\ \times 6 \\ \hline \end{array}$

2. $7\overline{)21}$ $\begin{array}{r} 7 \\ \times 3 \\ \hline \end{array}$ $3\overline{)21}$ $\begin{array}{r} 3 \\ \times 7 \\ \hline \end{array}$

3. $5\overline{)45}$ $\begin{array}{r} 5 \\ \times 9 \\ \hline \end{array}$ $9\overline{)45}$ $\begin{array}{r} 9 \\ \times 5 \\ \hline \end{array}$

4. $9\overline{)18}$ $\begin{array}{r} 9 \\ \times 2 \\ \hline \end{array}$ $2\overline{)18}$ $\begin{array}{r} 2 \\ \times 9 \\ \hline \end{array}$

5. $4\overline{)32}$ $\begin{array}{r} 4 \\ \times 8 \\ \hline \end{array}$ $8\overline{)32}$ $\begin{array}{r} 8 \\ \times 4 \\ \hline \end{array}$

6. A bagel shop bakes 72 bagels. There are 9 different kinds of bagels. If the bagel shop bakes the same number of each kind of bagel, how many of each kind do they bake? _____

7. Dr. Mackenzie wants to give each of his patients 2 toothbrushes. He has 16 patients today. How many toothbrushes will he give out? _____

8. Autumn has 36 watermelon seeds. She wants to split up the seeds evenly among her 4 friends. How many seeds will each friend get? _____

Division

49

Solve the following problems.

1 $2\overline{)18}$ $6\overline{)12}$ $7\overline{)21}$ $9\overline{)27}$ $5\overline{)40}$ $3\overline{)18}$

2 $3\overline{)15}$ $7\overline{)42}$ $6\overline{)24}$ $4\overline{)32}$ $3\overline{)27}$ $2\overline{)16}$

3 $9\overline{)63}$ $8\overline{)40}$ $5\overline{)20}$ $8\overline{)64}$ $4\overline{)28}$ $5\overline{)10}$

4 $8\overline{)24}$ $4\overline{)36}$ $3\overline{)21}$ $4\overline{)16}$ $9\overline{)54}$ $5\overline{)45}$

5 $2\overline{)12}$ $7\overline{)28}$ $8\overline{)32}$ $6\overline{)36}$ $7\overline{)56}$ $5\overline{)35}$

6 There are 45 marbles in a bag. Terrence wants to put these marbles in 5 equal groups. How many marbles will there be in each group? _____

7 There are 30 desks in the classroom. There are 6 rows of desks and each row has the same number of desks. How many desks are in each row? _____

8 The art teacher has 14 sets of paints. Each student gets 2 sets. How many students are in the class? _____

Division

50

Solve the following problems.

1. $8\overline{)56}$ $2\overline{)14}$ $7\overline{)35}$ $9\overline{)36}$ $4\overline{)20}$ $5\overline{)15}$

2. $6\overline{)42}$ $3\overline{)12}$ $9\overline{)81}$ $6\overline{)54}$ $5\overline{)30}$ $2\overline{)10}$

3. $9\overline{)45}$ $7\overline{)14}$ $5\overline{)25}$ $7\overline{)63}$ $6\overline{)18}$ $9\overline{)72}$

4. $3\overline{)24}$ $6\overline{)48}$ $4\overline{)24}$ $8\overline{)16}$ $6\overline{)30}$ $9\overline{)18}$

5. $2\overline{)12}$ $8\overline{)48}$ $8\overline{)72}$ $6\overline{)36}$ $3\overline{)21}$ $7\overline{)56}$

6. There are 72 third graders at Terry Elementary. There are 8 lunch tables. How many third graders sit at each table? _____

7. Marcy is on a trip and wants to visit 24 towns in 8 days. She plans to visit the same number of towns each day. How many towns can she visit each day? _____

8. There are 21 fish in Carly's backyard pond. Carly is moving to another house with 3 smaller ponds. If she puts the same number of fish in each, how many will she put in each pond? _____

Name _____

Take a Test Drive

Fill in the bubble beside the correct answer.

1 What number is skip counted here?
3, 6, 9, 12
- ○ 2
- ○ 3
- ○ 4
- ○ 6

2 Which shows skip counting by 5?
- ○ 2, 4, 6, 8, 10
- ○ 5, 6, 7, 8, 9
- ○ 5, 10, 15, 20, 25
- ○ 10, 20, 30, 40, 50

3 $7 \times 0 =$ _____
- ○ 0
- ○ 1
- ○ 7
- ○ 14

4 $2 \times 8 =$ _____
- ○ 2
- ○ 4
- ○ 8
- ○ 16

5
$$\begin{array}{r} 10 \\ \times\ 9 \\ \hline \end{array}$$
- ○ 0
- ○ 9
- ○ 19
- ○ 90

6
$$\begin{array}{r} 7 \\ \times 5 \\ \hline \end{array}$$
- ○ 2
- ○ 12
- ○ 15
- ○ 35

7 Outside the barn at Jim's Stables is an apple tree. 42 apples have fallen to the ground. Jim wants to divide them equally among his 6 horses. How many apples will each horse get to eat?
- ○ 7
- ○ 6
- ○ 5
- ○ 4

8 If there are 9 carrots to divide equally among 3 rabbits, how many will each rabbit get?
- ○ 2
- ○ 3
- ○ 6
- ○ 9

Name _____

Take a Test Drive

Fill in the bubble beside the correct answer.

---

1 $10 \div 2 =$ _____
- ◯ 5
- ◯ 8
- ◯ 12
- ◯ 20

---

2 $40 \div 10 =$ _____
- ◯ 1
- ◯ 4
- ◯ 10
- ◯ 50

---

3   Which problem could you use to check this equation? $3 \times 5 = 15$
- ◯ $3 + 5 = 8$
- ◯ $5 - 3 = 2$
- ◯ $15 \div 3 = 5$
- ◯ $5 \times 2 = 10$

---

4   Which problem could you use to check this equation? $24 \div 6 = 4$
- ◯ $4 + 6 = 10$
- ◯ $6 - 4 = 2$
- ◯ $24 \div 3 = 8$
- ◯ $4 \times 6 = 24$

---

5   Which equation is the same as this one? $12 \div 2 = 6$
- ◯ $\frac{6}{2} = 3$
- ◯ $\begin{array}{r} 6 \\ \times 2 \\ \hline 12 \end{array}$
- ◯ $2\overline{)12}^{\,6}$
- ◯ $4\overline{)12}^{\,3}$

---

6   Which equation is the same as this one? $4\overline{)8}^{\,2}$
- ◯ $4 \div 2 = 2$
- ◯ $24 \div 8 = 3$
- ◯ $8 \div 4 = 2$
- ◯ $8 \times 4 = 32$

---

7 $25 \div 5 =$ _____
- ◯ 1
- ◯ 5
- ◯ 20
- ◯ 25

---

8 $8 \div 4 =$ _____
- ◯ 1
- ◯ 2
- ◯ 4
- ◯ 32

Fractions

53

⭐ Fractions can tell about 1 whole divided into smaller pieces. This circle is divided into 4 equal parts. 1 part is shaded.

$\frac{1}{4}$ - how many parts are shaded
- how many parts in all

Draw a line to match the fraction with the shape.

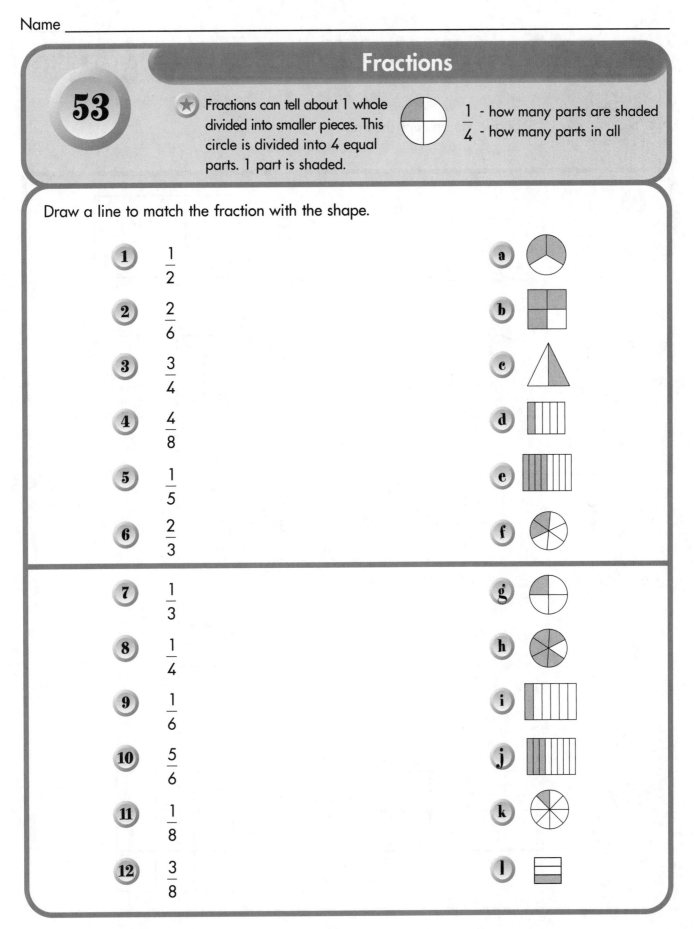

1. $\frac{1}{2}$

2. $\frac{2}{6}$

3. $\frac{3}{4}$

4. $\frac{4}{8}$

5. $\frac{1}{5}$

6. $\frac{2}{3}$

7. $\frac{1}{3}$

8. $\frac{1}{4}$

9. $\frac{1}{6}$

10. $\frac{5}{6}$

11. $\frac{1}{8}$

12. $\frac{3}{8}$

a

b

c

d

e

f

g

h

i

j

k

l

Name _____

Fractions

54

Shade the amount shown.

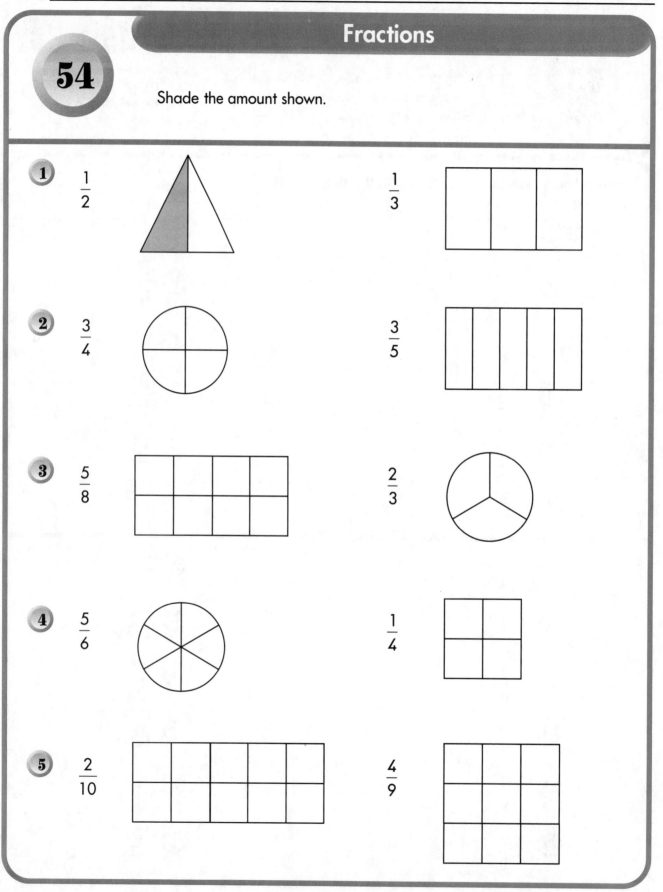

1. $\frac{1}{2}$ $\frac{1}{3}$

2. $\frac{3}{4}$ $\frac{3}{5}$

3. $\frac{5}{8}$ $\frac{2}{3}$

4. $\frac{5}{6}$ $\frac{1}{4}$

5. $\frac{2}{10}$ $\frac{4}{9}$

Advantage Math Grade 3 © 2004 Creative Teaching Press

Name _____

Name Fractions

55

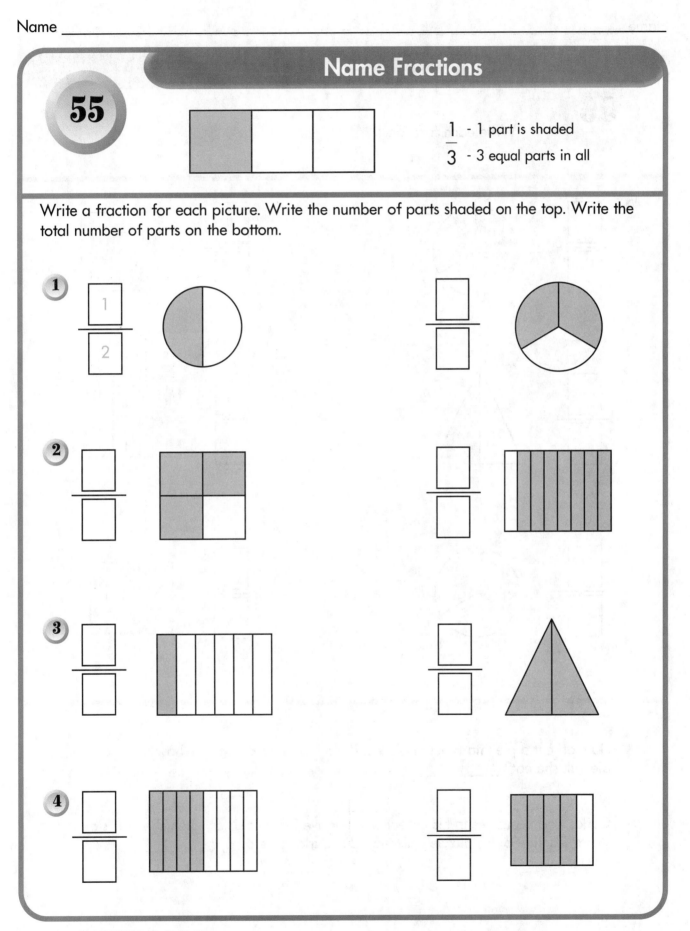

$\dfrac{1}{3}$ - 1 part is shaded
- 3 equal parts in all

Write a fraction for each picture. Write the number of parts shaded on the top. Write the total number of parts on the bottom.

Name Fractions

56

Write each fraction.

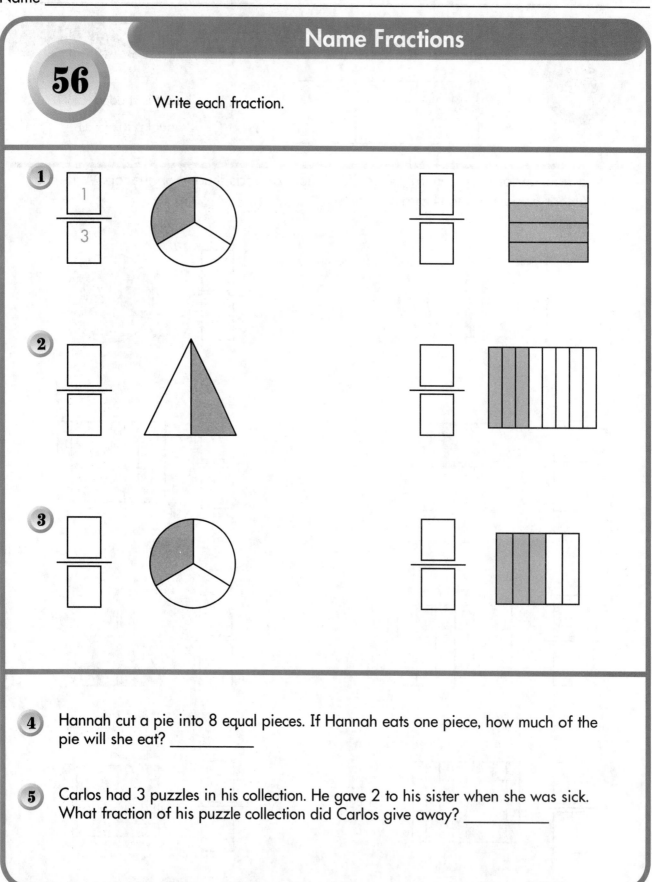

1.

$\dfrac{1}{3}$

2.

3.

4. Hannah cut a pie into 8 equal pieces. If Hannah eats one piece, how much of the pie will she eat? _____

5. Carlos had 3 puzzles in his collection. He gave 2 to his sister when she was sick. What fraction of his puzzle collection did Carlos give away? _____

Name _____

Compare Fractions

57

⭐ Use these symbols to compare numbers:
= equals
< is less than
> is greater than

$\dfrac{3}{4}$ > $\dfrac{1}{4}$

When fractions have the same bottom number,
compare them by looking at the numbers on the top.

Complete the number sentence with =, <, or >.

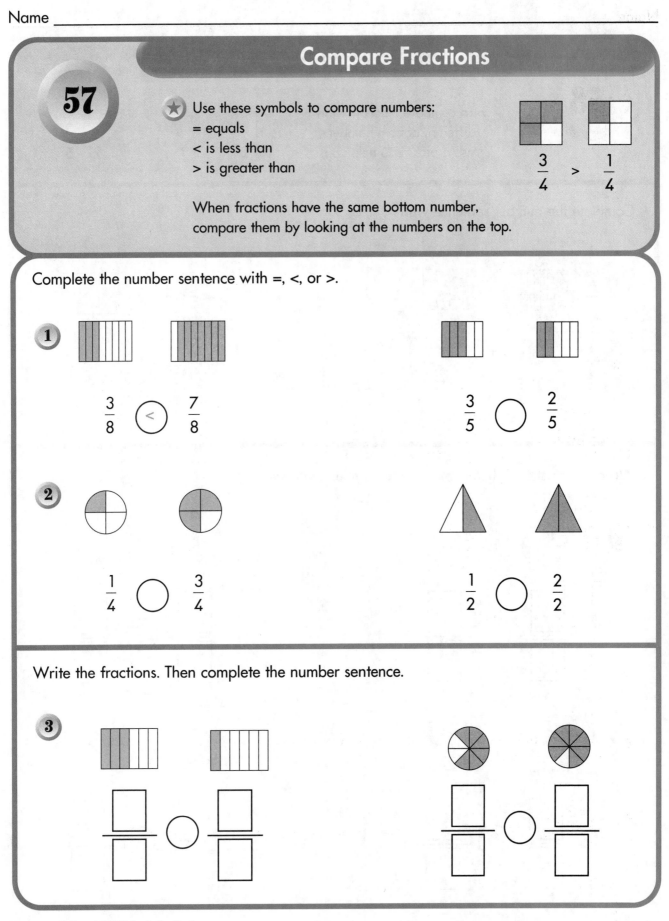

1 $\dfrac{3}{8}$ ◯< $\dfrac{7}{8}$ $\dfrac{3}{5}$ ◯ $\dfrac{2}{5}$

2 $\dfrac{1}{4}$ ◯ $\dfrac{3}{4}$ $\dfrac{1}{2}$ ◯ $\dfrac{2}{2}$

Write the fractions. Then complete the number sentence.

3

Compare Fractions

58

$$\frac{1}{2} = \frac{3}{6}$$

Complete the number sentence with =, <, or >.

1

$$\frac{3}{8} \;\text{\textless}\; \frac{3}{4}$$

$$\frac{2}{6} \;\bigcirc\; \frac{1}{3}$$

Write the fractions. Then complete the number sentence.

2

$$\frac{\square}{\square} \;\bigcirc\; \frac{\square}{\square}$$

$$\frac{\square}{\square} \;\bigcirc\; \frac{\square}{\square}$$

3

$$\frac{\square}{\square} \;\bigcirc\; \frac{\square}{\square}$$

$$\frac{\square}{\square} \;\bigcirc\; \frac{\square}{\square}$$

Decimals

59

★ Decimal numbers are another way to show part of a whole. Numbers after the decimal point tell about amounts smaller than a whole. 0.34 is smaller than 1.0.

$$\frac{3}{10} = .3 = 0.3$$

All of these numbers are three-tenths.

Write how many parts are shaded using a decimal number.

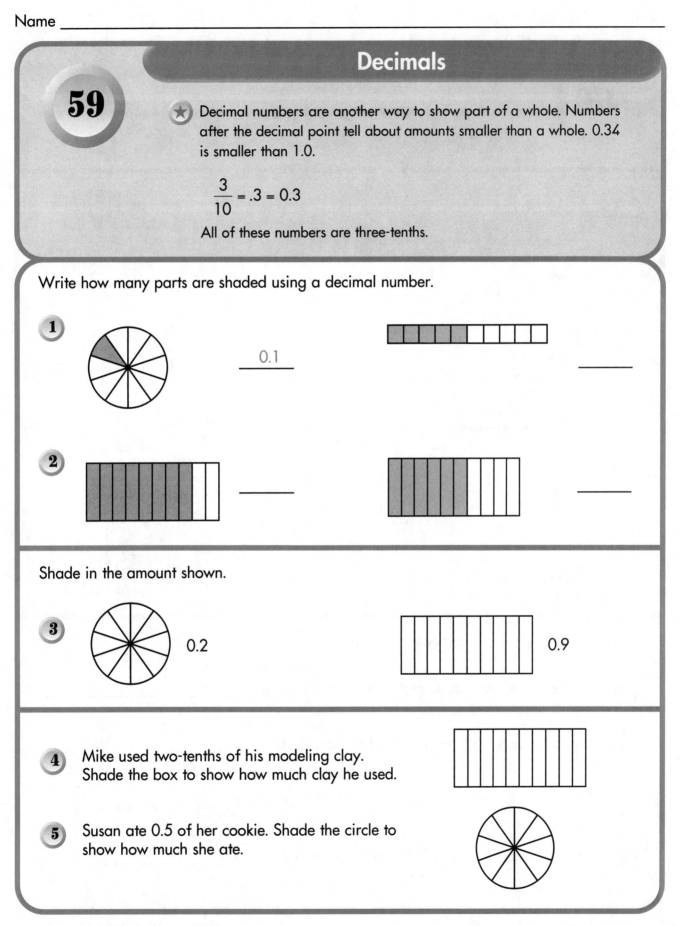

1   0.1

2   _____

Shade in the amount shown.

3   0.2   0.9

4   Mike used two-tenths of his modeling clay.
     Shade the box to show how much clay he used.

5   Susan ate 0.5 of her cookie. Shade the circle to
     show how much she ate.

Decimals

60

Write the letter of the matching picture next to the number word or number.

_____ ① 0.4

_____ ② 0.7

_____ ③ 0.0

_____ ④ three-tenths

_____ ⑤ eight-tenths

_____ ⑥ two-tenths

a

b

c

d

e

f

Write a word or phrase to answer the question.

⑦ What coin can you use to make $0.01 or one cent? _____

⑧ How many dollar bills do you need to make $1.00? _____

⑨ What one coin can you use to make $0.10 or ten cents? _____

⑩ How many quarters ($0.25) do you need to make $1.00? _____

Decimals

61

⭐ Where a digit appears in a number determines its value.

3 . 2 6
ones tenths hundredths

five-hundredths = $\frac{5}{100}$ = .05 = 0.05

Five out of 100 parts are shaded.

Write how many parts are shaded using a decimal number.

1 _0.35_ _____ _____

Shade in the amount shown.

2 0.16   0.51   0.89

3 1.00   0.20   0.75

Decimals

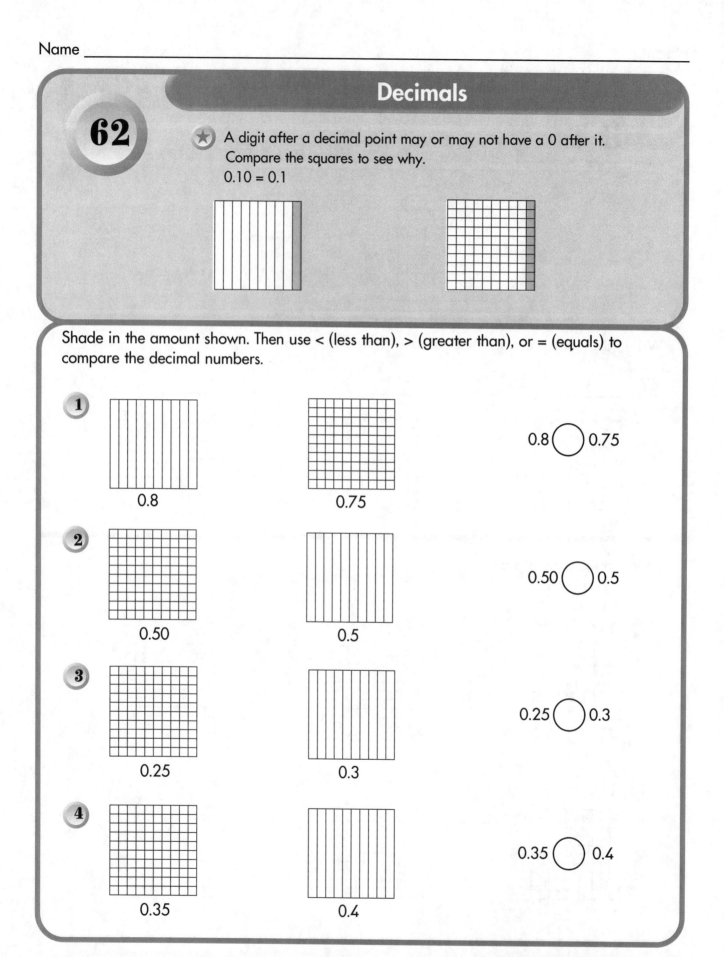

62

⭐ A digit after a decimal point may or may not have a 0 after it. Compare the squares to see why.

0.10 = 0.1

Shade in the amount shown. Then use < (less than), > (greater than), or = (equals) to compare the decimal numbers.

1. 0.8   0.75   0.8 ◯ 0.75

2. 0.50   0.5   0.50 ◯ 0.5

3. 0.25   0.3   0.25 ◯ 0.3

4. 0.35   0.4   0.35 ◯ 0.4

Name _____

Take a Test Drive

Fill in the bubble beside the correct answer.

1 What fraction of the shape is shaded?

○ $\frac{1}{3}$ ○ $\frac{1}{2}$

○ $\frac{2}{3}$ ○ $\frac{2}{2}$

2 What fraction of the shape is shaded?

○ $\frac{1}{4}$ ○ $\frac{1}{5}$

○ $\frac{1}{2}$ ○ $\frac{4}{5}$

3 What fraction of the shape is shaded?

○ $\frac{1}{3}$ ○ $\frac{2}{2}$

○ $\frac{3}{3}$ ○ $\frac{3}{4}$

4 Which shape has $\frac{1}{2}$ of its parts shaded?

○   ○

○   ○

5 Which shape has $\frac{3}{4}$ of its parts shaded?

○   ○

○   ○

6 Which shape has $\frac{5}{8}$ of its parts shaded?

○   ○

○   ○

7 Rachel had five sticks of gum. She chewed two sticks. What fraction of her gum did she chew?

○ $\frac{3}{2}$ ○ $\frac{5}{2}$

○ $\frac{2}{5}$ ○ $\frac{2}{3}$

8 Zack had a pack of 10 crayons. If he used 5 of them, how much of the pack did he use?

○ 5

○ 0.5

○ 0.05

○ 5.5

Name _____

Take a Test Drive

Fill in the bubble beside the correct answer.

1

$\frac{3}{5} \bigcirc \frac{2}{5}$

- ○ <
- ○ >
- ○ =
- ○ +

---

5 How much of the shape is shaded?

- ○ 0.10
- ○ 0.21
- ○ 0.26
- ○ 0.30

---

2 Which fraction completes the number sentence $\frac{4}{7} <$

- ○ $\frac{6}{7}$
- ○ $\frac{3}{7}$
- ○ $\frac{1}{7}$
- ○ $\frac{0}{7}$

---

6 Which number sentence tells about the picture?

- ○ 7 < 75
- ○ 0.7 > 0.75
- ○ 0.7 < 0.75
- ○ 0.7 = 0.75

---

3 Which number sentence tells about the picture?

- ○ $\frac{2}{3} > \frac{1}{3}$
- ○ $\frac{2}{6} > \frac{1}{3}$
- ○ $\frac{1}{3} < \frac{2}{6}$
- ○ $\frac{2}{6} = \frac{1}{3}$

---

7 Which coin is worth $0.01?

- ○
- ○
- ○
- ○

---

4 How much of the shape is shaded?

- ○ 0.3
- ○ 0.4
- ○ 0.10
- ○ 0.04

---

8 Which coin is worth $0.10?

- ○
- ○
- ○
- ○

Telling Time

65

⭐ There are 5 minutes between each hour mark.
Write the minutes on the clock by 5's.

$$6:40$$

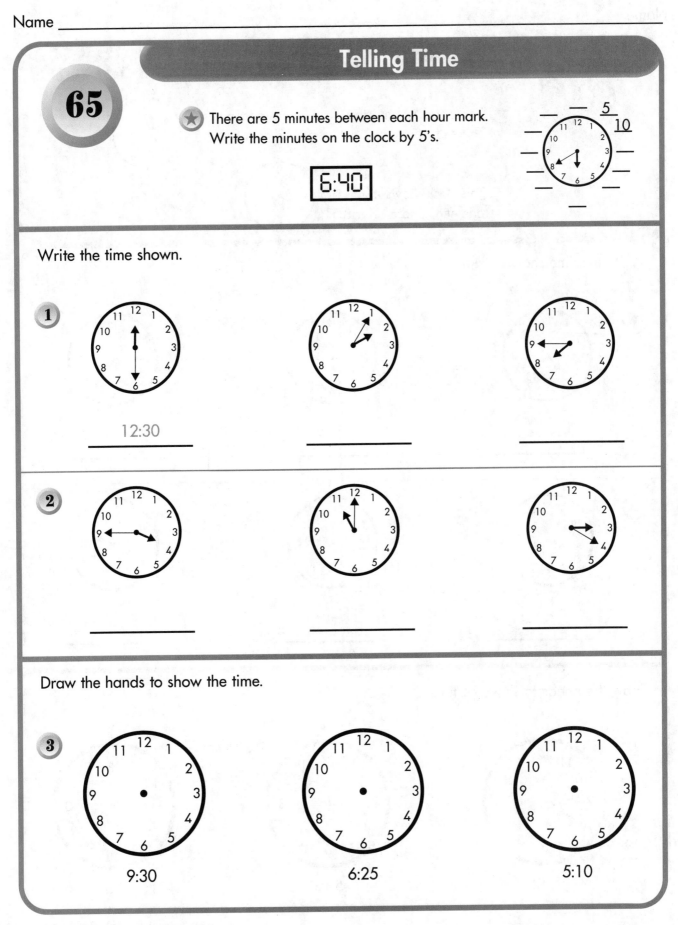

Write the time shown.

1

12:30

_____   _____   _____

2

_____   _____   _____

Draw the hands to show the time.

3

9:30   6:25   5:10

Telling Time

66

⭐ Each mark on the clock face means one minute.
There are 5 minutes between each hour mark.

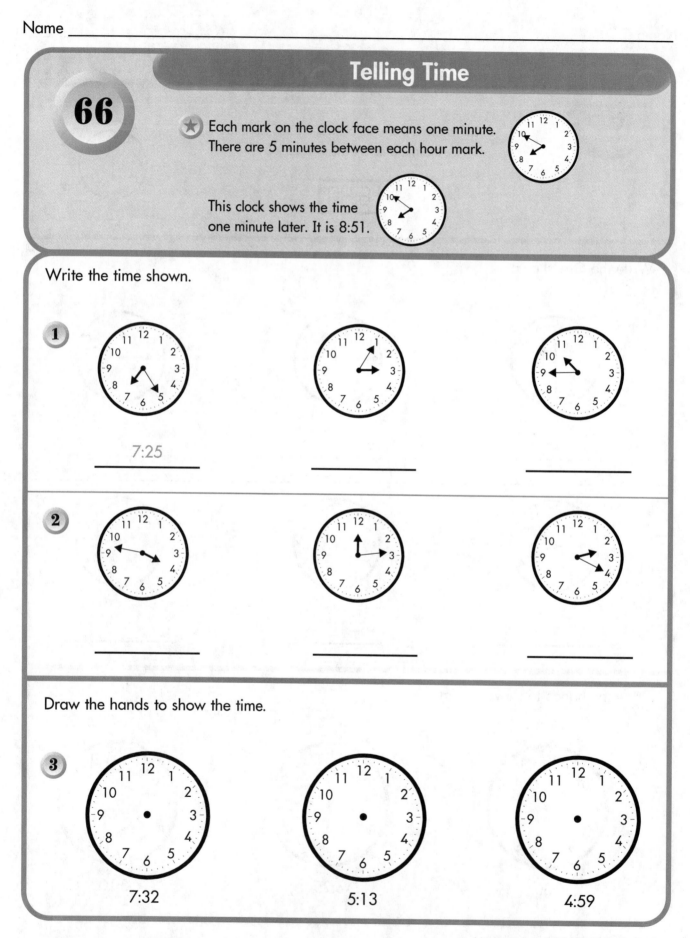

This clock shows the time
one minute later. It is 8:51.

Write the time shown.

1

7:25

_____   _____   _____

2

_____   _____   _____

Draw the hands to show the time.

3

7:32   5:13   4:59

Name _____

67

⭐ Clock hands move as time moves on.

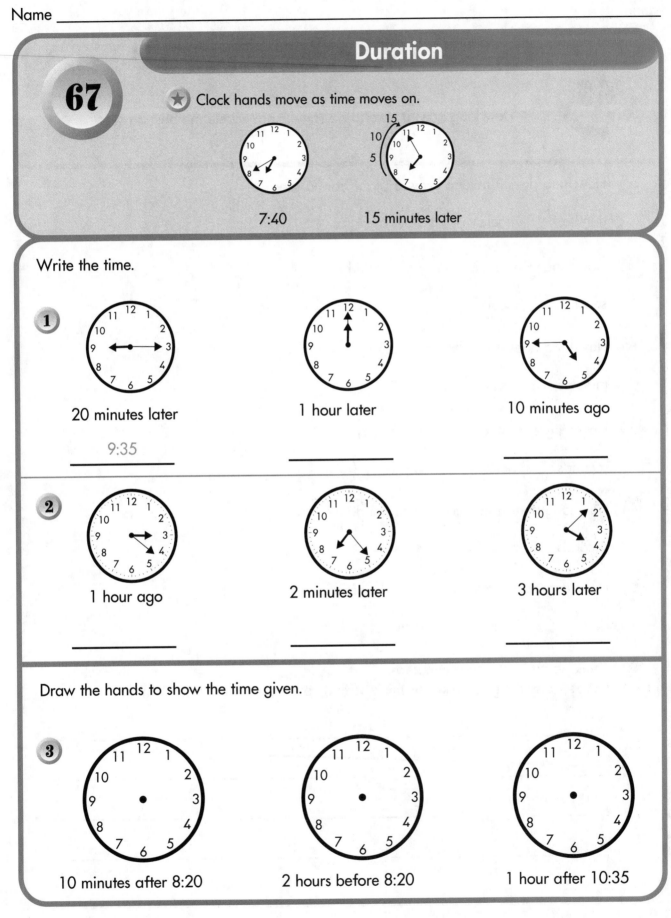

7:40   15 minutes later

Write the time.

1

20 minutes later   1 hour later   10 minutes ago

9:35   _____   _____

2

1 hour ago   2 minutes later   3 hours later

_____   _____   _____

Draw the hands to show the time given.

3

10 minutes after 8:20   2 hours before 8:20   1 hour after 10:35

Duration

68

How long does it take to do something? Circle the best answer.

1 How long does it take to grow a plant from a seed?

minute   hours   days

2 How long does it take to say the alphabet?

seconds   hours   days

3 How long does it take to get to school?

minutes   days   weeks

4 How long does it take for a tooth to grow in?

seconds   hours   weeks

5 How long does it take to walk to the door?

seconds   hours   days

6 How long does it take for a baby to grow up?

days   weeks   years

7 Think about how long a minute is.
List as many things as you can think of that you could do in about 1 minute.

_____

_____

_____

_____

Counting Money

69

1 penny = 1¢ or $0.01	1 nickel = 5¢ or $0.05	1 dime = 10¢ or $0.10	1 quarter = 25¢ or $0.25

Write the amount of money.

1.   <u>5</u>   <u>10</u>   <u>11</u>   = <u>11</u> ¢

2.   ____ ____ ____ ____ ____   = _____ ¢

3.   ____ ____ ____ ____   = _____ ¢

4.   ____ ____ ____ ____ ____ ____   = _____ ¢

5.   ____ ____ ____ ____ ____   = _____ ¢

6.   ____ ____ ____ ____ ____ ____ ____   = _____ ¢

Counting Money

70

⭐ 99¢ is the same as $0.99.
When you have more than $0.99, you have $1.00 or more.

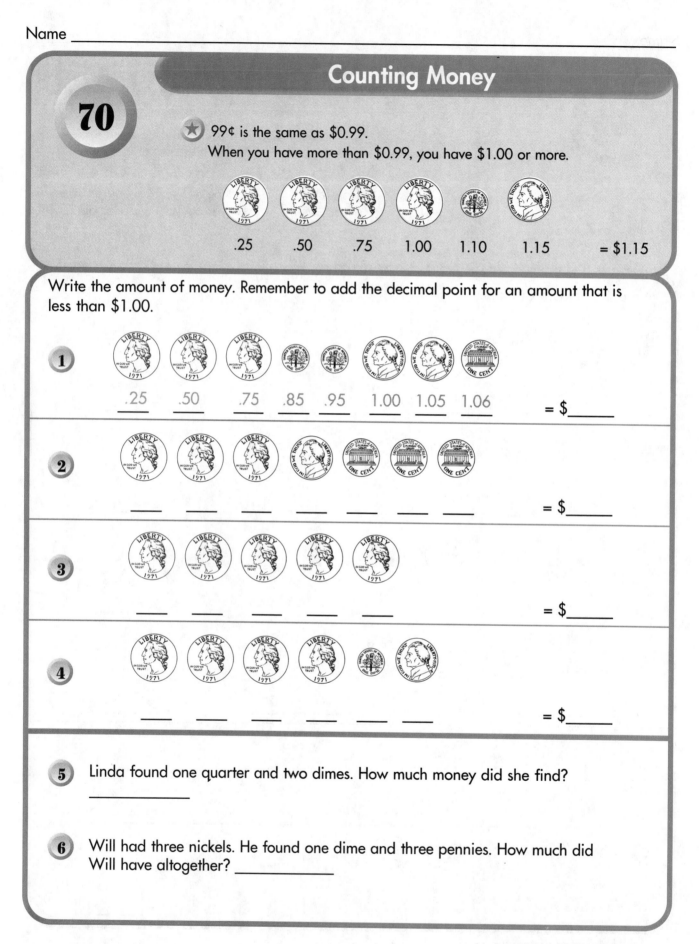

.25   .50   .75   1.00   1.10   1.15   = $1.15

Write the amount of money. Remember to add the decimal point for an amount that is less than $1.00.

1   .25   .50   .75   .85   .95   1.00   1.05   1.06   = $_____

2   ____ ____ ____ ____ ____ ____ ____   = $_____

3   ____ ____ ____ ____ ____   = $_____

4   ____ ____ ____ ____ ____   = $_____

5 Linda found one quarter and two dimes. How much money did she find?
_____

6 Will had three nickels. He found one dime and three pennies. How much did Will have altogether? _____

Adding Money

71

⭐ Adding money is just like regular adding. Just remember to keep the decimal points lined up.

Jeff bought 1 ball and 1 bat. How much did Jeff pay?

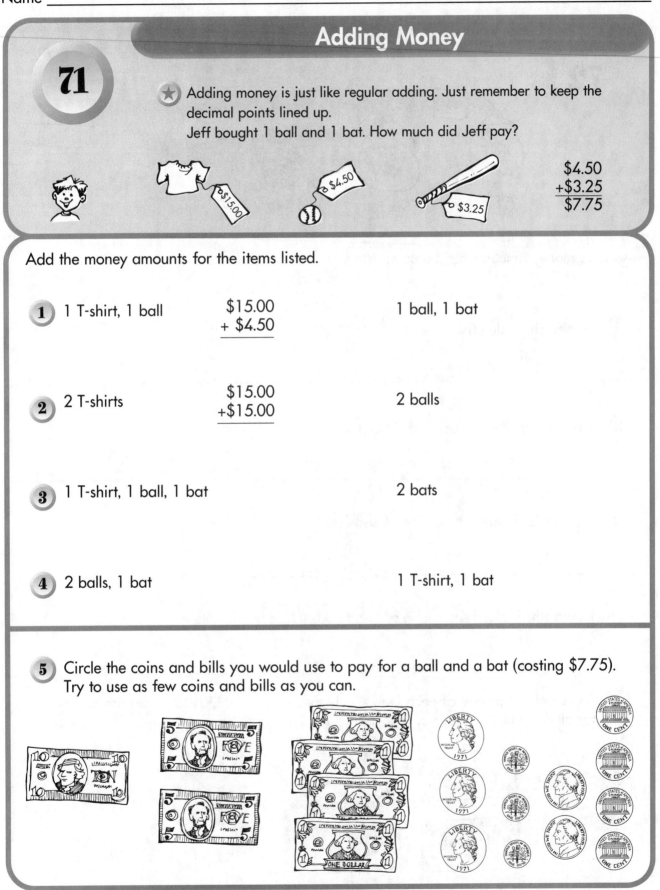

$4.50
+$3.25
$7.75

Add the money amounts for the items listed.

1 1 T-shirt, 1 ball $15.00
                              + $4.50   1 ball, 1 bat

2 2 T-shirts $15.00
                             +$15.00   2 balls

3 1 T-shirt, 1 ball, 1 bat   2 bats

4 2 balls, 1 bat   1 T-shirt, 1 bat

5 Circle the coins and bills you would use to pay for a ball and a bat (costing $7.75).
Try to use as few coins and bills as you can.

Name _____

72

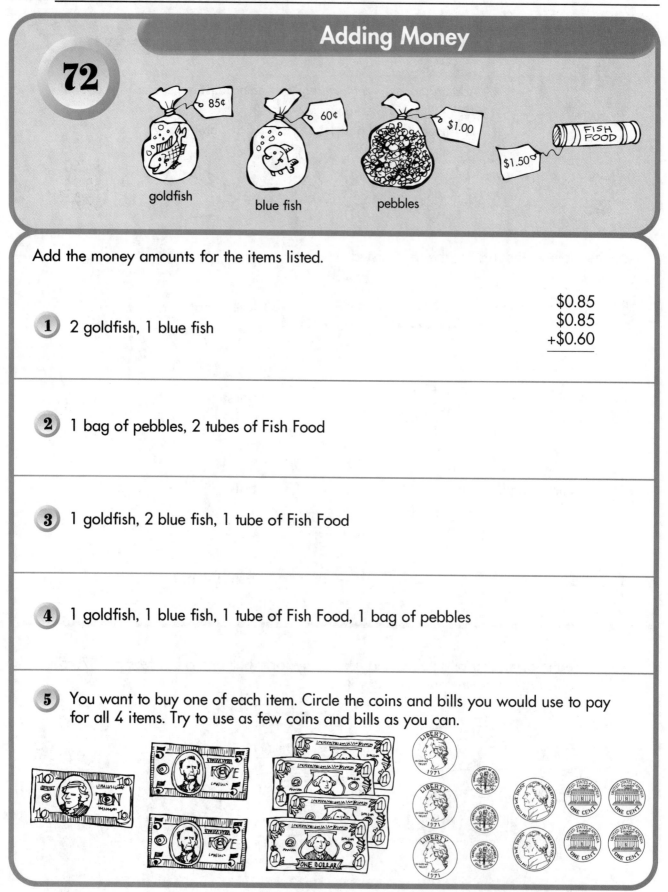

85¢ goldfish

60¢ blue fish

$1.00 pebbles

$1.50 FISH FOOD

Add the money amounts for the items listed.

1 2 goldfish, 1 blue fish

$0.85
$0.85
+$0.60
———

2 1 bag of pebbles, 2 tubes of Fish Food

3 1 goldfish, 2 blue fish, 1 tube of Fish Food

4 1 goldfish, 1 blue fish, 1 tube of Fish Food, 1 bag of pebbles

5 You want to buy one of each item. Circle the coins and bills you would use to pay for all 4 items. Try to use as few coins and bills as you can.

Subtracting Money

73

bought gum for $0.60. If he paid with $5.00, how much change will he get back?

$$\begin{array}{r} \$5.00 \\ -\$0.60 \\ \hline \$4.40 \end{array}$$

60¢   50¢ $1.00 $1.35

GUM

Find the change by subtracting the total cost from $5.00.

1 bought 1 ball

2 bought 1 bag of marbles

3 bought 1 toy car

4 bought 1 toy car and 1 bag of marbles

5 bought 1 toy car and 1 ball

6 bought 2 cars and 1 pack of gum

7 bought 1 ball, 1 pack of gum, and 1 bag of marbles

Subtracting Money

74

HOT DOG . . . . . $1.75   JUICE $1.05
HAMBURGER . . . . $2.00   BOTTLED
FRIES . . . . $0.75   WATER $0.90

Read the story problem. Add the amounts to find the price. Subtract the price from the amount each person has.

1 Juan bought a hot dog and water for lunch.
He paid $3.00. How much change will he get
back? _____

2 Ryan bought a hamburger, fries, and juice.
He paid $4.00. How much change will he get
back? _____

3 Kayla and Anna wanted to buy a hot dog, a
hamburger, juice, and water. They have
$5.00. Do they have enough money? _____

4 If Kayla and Anna have enough to buy all they wanted, how much
change will they get back (if any)? If not, how much more do they
need? (Hint: If they had enough, subtract the price from their $5.00. If they didn't
have enough, subtract their $5.00 from the price.) _____

5 Sara has $4.00. She wants a hamburger, fries,
and water. Does she have enough money?
_____

6 If Sara has enough to buy all she wants, how
much change will she get back (if any)? If not,
how much more does she need? _____

75

Take a Test Drive

Fill in the bubble beside the correct answer.

1 What time does the clock show?

○ 2:00
○ 2:20
○ 4:10
○ 4:30

2 What time does the clock show?

○ 8:40
○ 9:00
○ 9:42
○ 10:45

3 Which clock shows 11:10?

○
○
○
○

4 What time will it be 20 minutes from the time shown?

○ 4:05
○ 4:35
○ 4:25
○ 5:15

5 What time was it 2 hours ago?

○ 10:55
○ 12:55
○ 1:45
○ 1:35

6 About how long does it take to walk around the block?

○ minutes
○ hours
○ days
○ weeks

7 About how long does it take a tree to grow as tall as a house?

○ minutes
○ hours
○ years
○ weeks

8 About how long does it take to watch a baseball game?

○ minutes
○ hours
○ days
○ weeks

Name _____

Take a Test Drive

Fill in the bubble beside the correct answer.

---

1 How much money is this?

- ○ 6¢
- ○ 33¢
- ○ 57¢
- ○ 58¢

---

5 $2.60
     +$4.36

- ○ $2.26
- ○ $6.96
- ○ $7.96
- ○ $8.36

---

2 Which amount does NOT equal $0.20?

- ○
- ○
- ○
- ○

---

6 $4.00
     −$2.25

- ○ $1.75
- ○ $2.25
- ○ $2.75
- ○ $6.25

---

3 How much money is this?

- ○ $1.02
- ○ $1.26
- ○ $2.30
- ○ $2255

---

7 Lauren had one quarter, two dimes, and four pennies. How much money did she have altogether?

- ○ 7 cents
- ○ 49 cents
- ○ 54 cents
- ○ 74 cents

---

4 $3.50
     +$0.95

- ○ $2.55
- ○ $3.45
- ○ $4.45
- ○ $5.00

---

8 Thomas bought a notebook for $1.25. He gave the cashier $2.00. How much change should he get back?

- ○ $0.75
- ○ $1.75
- ○ $2.00
- ○ $3.25

Name _____

77 ⭐ Plane figures are flat, closed shapes. Angles are where two sides meet.

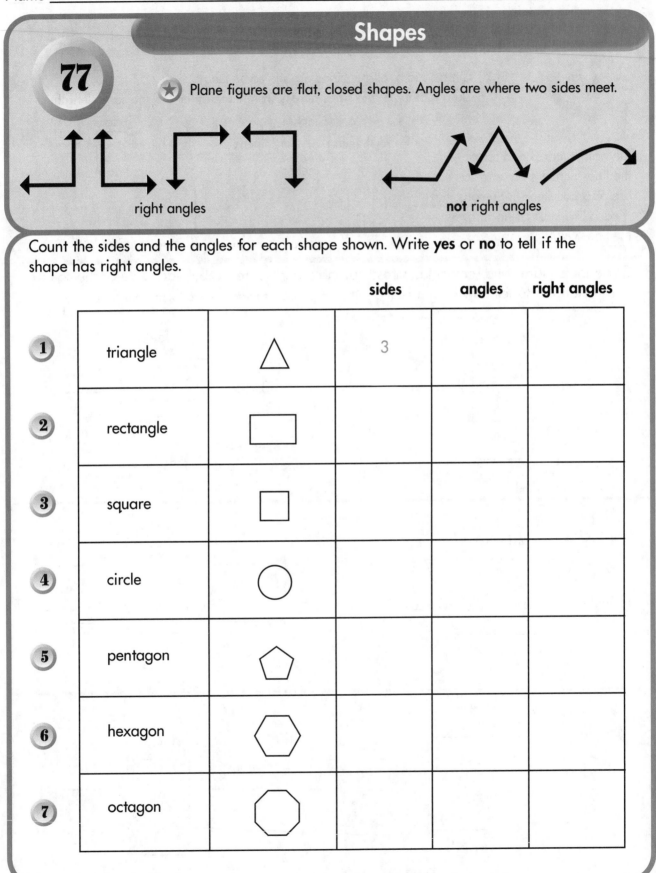

right angles   **not** right angles

Count the sides and the angles for each shape shown. Write **yes** or **no** to tell if the shape has right angles.

			sides	angles	right angles
1	triangle	△	3		
2	rectangle	▭			
3	square	▢			
4	circle	◯			
5	pentagon	⬠			
6	hexagon	⬡			
7	octagon	⯃			

Shakes

 78

⭐ On a square, all the sides are the same length.
On a rectangle, the sides across from each other are the same length.

On both squares and rectangles, the lines across from each other are also parallel. That means that if each line kept going forever, the lines would never meet.

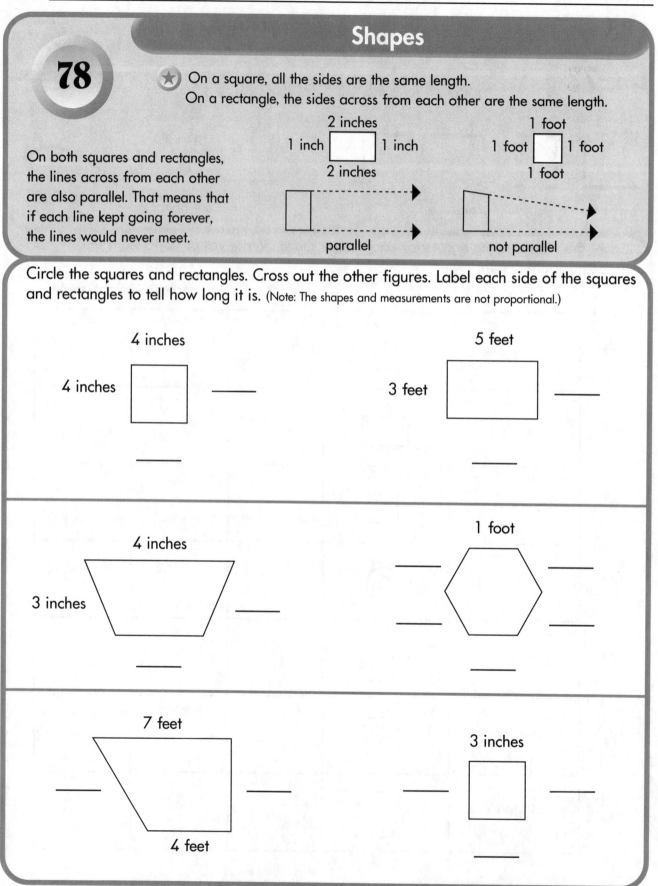

Circle the squares and rectangles. Cross out the other figures. Label each side of the squares and rectangles to tell how long it is. (Note: The shapes and measurements are not proportional.)

Shapes—Triangles

79 ⭐ There are many types of triangles. All of them have three sides and three angles.
Right Triangle—has a right angle.

Isosceles Triangle—2 sides are equal in length.

Equilateral Triangle—all 3 sides are equal in length.

Color the right triangles red. Color the isosceles triangles blue. Color the equilateral triangles yellow.

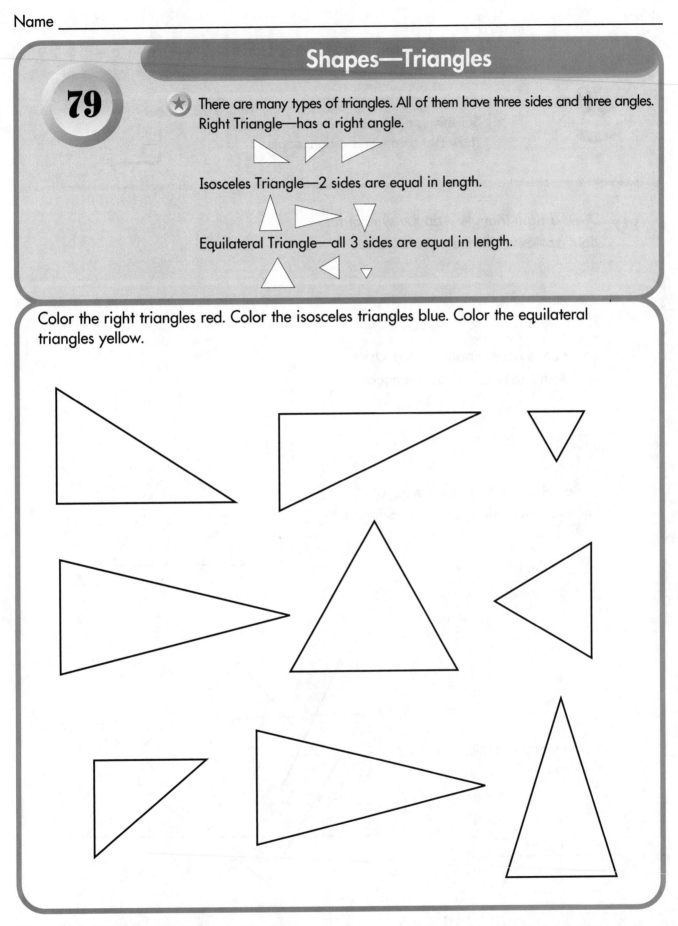

Name _____

80

★ Sometimes a diagram will use a symbol to show that an angle is a right angle.

1 Draw a right triangle. Add the symbol for right angles where the right angle is.

2 Draw an isosceles triangle. Hint: Use a ruler to make sure 2 sides are equal.

3 Use a ruler to measure the sides of the equilateral triangle. Label each side.

4 How many triangles do you see?

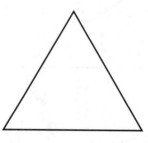

_____

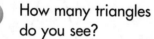

Solid Shapes

81

⭐ Solid shapes are wide, long, and tall.

A ball is not a circle but a **sphere.**

A block is not a square but a **cube.**

A box is not a rectangle but a **rectangular prism.**

Look at the solid shape. Tell what flat shapes are part of it.

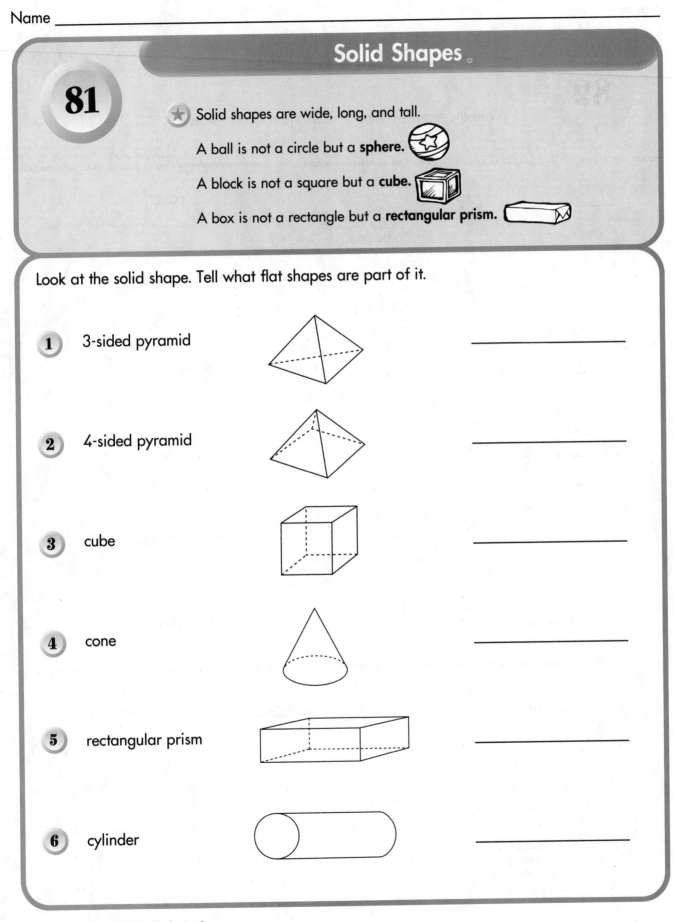

1. 3-sided pyramid   _____

2. 4-sided pyramid   _____

3. cube   _____

4. cone   _____

5. rectangular prism   _____

6. cylinder   _____

Solid Shapes

82

Write the letter of the name of the shape beside it.

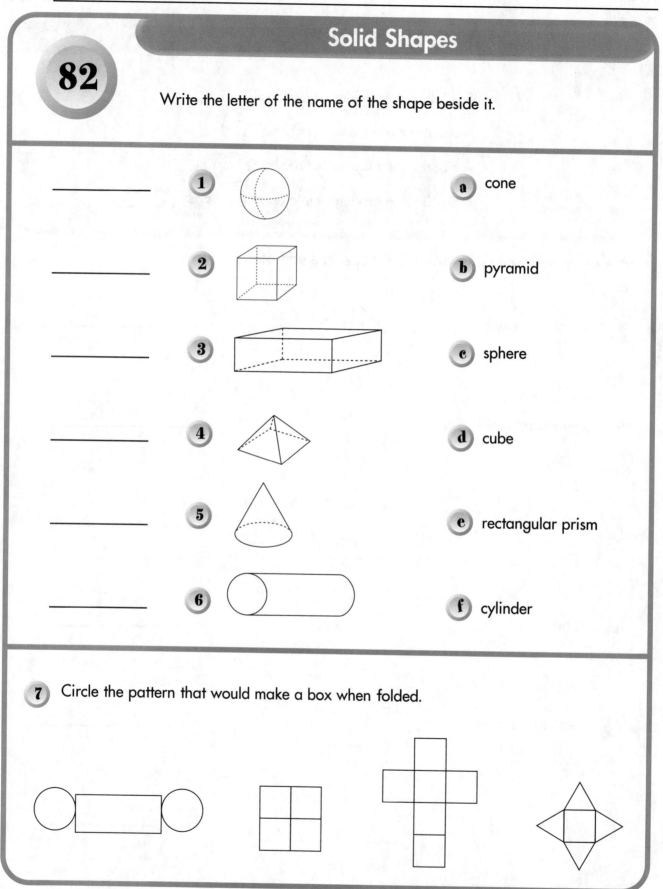

_____ **1**   **a** cone

_____ **2**   **b** pyramid

_____ **3**   **c** sphere

_____ **4**   **d** cube

_____ **5**   **e** rectangular prism

_____ **6**   **f** cylinder

7 Circle the pattern that would make a box when folded.

Measurements

83

⭐ Time is measured with a clock or calendar in minutes, hours, days, and weeks. Length is measured with a ruler in inches, feet, yards, and miles. Weight is measured with a scale in ounces, pounds, and tons.

Write **time, length,** or **weight** to tell how to measure the item.

1 how tall you are _____

2 how long it takes to mow the lawn _____

3 how heavy your dog is _____

4 how light a feather is _____

5 how far it is around your yard _____

6 how long it takes to put dishes away _____

7 how wide your kitchen counter is _____

8 how heavy this book is _____

9 Susan's history book weighs 2.5 pounds. Her math book weighs 2 pounds. How much more does the history book weigh? _____

10 Kevin studied for a test. He spent 25 minutes reading, 20 minutes taking notes, and 32 minutes reviewing his notes. How much time did he spend studying? _____

Measurements

84

⭐ In the U.S. customary system, length is measured using inches, feet, and miles. The metric system measures length using centimeters, meters, and kilometers.

Write **inches, feet,** or **miles** to show the best U.S. customary system measurement for the item.

1 your finger _____   a road between two cities _____

2 a city block _____   a car _____

3 a highway _____   a pencil _____

4 a baby _____   a railroad track between two stations _____

Write **centimeters, meters,** or **kilometers** to show the best metric system measurement for the item.

5 your finger _____   a road between two cities _____

6 a city block _____   a car _____

7 a highway _____   a pencil _____

8 a baby _____   a railroad track between two stations _____

Measure Length

85

⭐ A ruler gives an exact measurement of length, width, and height.

IN.   1   2   3   4

This line is 3½ inches long.

Use a ruler to measure the length of the line in inches.

1 ———————— _____

2 ———————————— _____

3 —————————————————— _____

4 ———— _____

⭐ This line is 9 centimeters long.

cm 1 2 3 4 5 6 7 8 9 10 11 12

Use a ruler to measure the length of the line in centimeters.

5 —————————— _____

6 ———————————————— _____

7 —————————————————————— _____

8 ———————————— _____

Measure Length

86

⭐ Estimating is like rounding. You decide what measurement something is closest to.

IN.   1   2   3   4

This line is about 2 inches long.

IN.   1   2   3   4

This line is about 4 inches long.

Use a ruler to measure the length of the line to the nearest inch.

1 _____   _____

2 _____   _____

3 _____   _____

4 _____   _____

Use a ruler to measure the length of the line to the nearest centimeter.

5 _____   _____

6 _____   _____

7 _____   _____

8 _____   _____

Perimeter

87

⭐ **Perimeter** is the distance around an object. Add each side to find the perimeter.

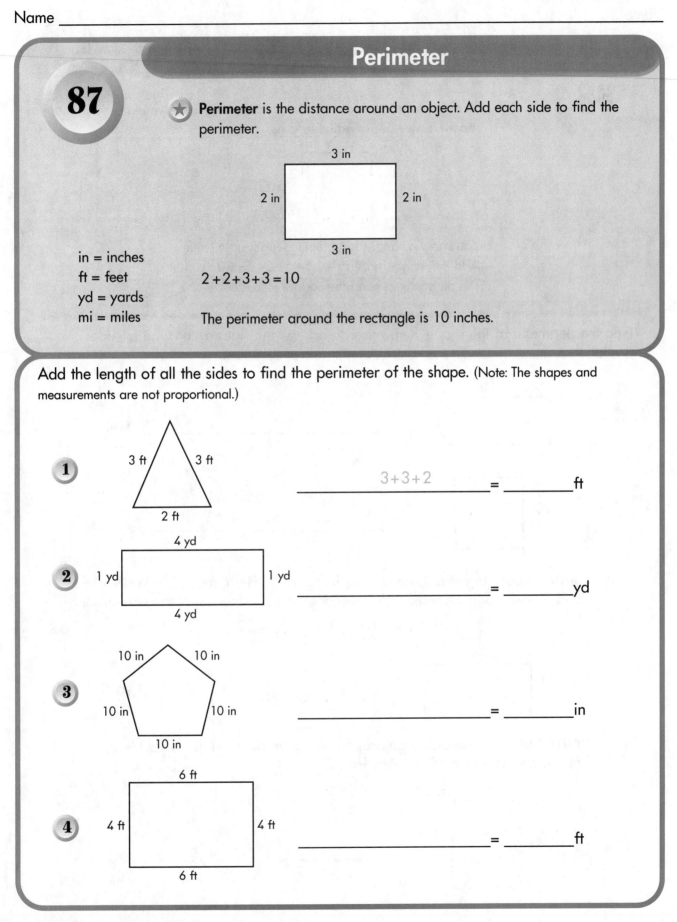

3 in

2 in   2 in

3 in

in = inches
ft = feet
yd = yards
mi = miles

$2+2+3+3=10$

The perimeter around the rectangle is 10 inches.

Add the length of all the sides to find the perimeter of the shape. (Note: The shapes and measurements are not proportional.)

1   3 ft   3 ft

2 ft

_____ 3+3+2 _____ = _____ ft

2   4 yd

1 yd   1 yd

4 yd

_____ = _____ yd

3   10 in   10 in

10 in   10 in

10 in

_____ = _____ in

4   6 ft

4 ft   4 ft

6 ft

_____ = _____ ft

Name _____

88

⭐ Sometimes not all sides are labeled on a shape. But you know that many shapes have sides of equal lengths.

5 ft ☐

You know a square is the same length on all sides.
Add the length of all sides: $5+5+5+5=20$
The perimeter around the square is 20 feet.

Find the perimeter of the shape. Remember to add all the sides even if not all sides are labeled. (Note: The shapes and measurements are not proportional.)

1 1 ft ▭ 5 ft

_____1+5+1+5_____ = _____ feet

2 9 in ☐

_____ = _____ inches

3 Jessica needs to put a fence around her garden. Her garden is 4 yards wide and 8 yards long. How much fencing does she need to go all the way around it?

4 yd ▭ 8 yd

_____8 + 4 + 8 + 4_____ = _____ yards

4 Austin bought a border to go around his room. His room is 15 feet long and 10 feet wide. How long will the border be?

15 ft ☐ 10 ft

_____ = _____ feet

Area and Volume

89

⭐ The **area** of a shape is the amount of space the shape covers. Find the area of a rectangular figure by multiplying the length times the width.

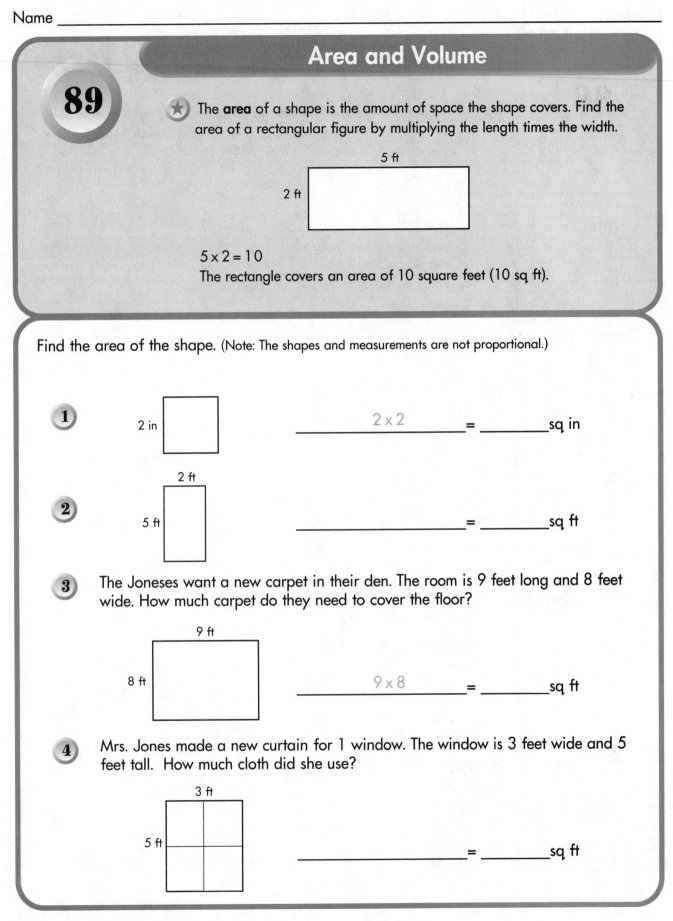

5 ft

2 ft

$5 \times 2 = 10$

The rectangle covers an area of 10 square feet (10 sq ft).

Find the area of the shape. (Note: The shapes and measurements are not proportional.)

1 2 in   _____2 × 2_____ = _____ sq in

2 2 ft
       5 ft   _____ = _____ sq ft

3 The Joneses want a new carpet in their den. The room is 9 feet long and 8 feet wide. How much carpet do they need to cover the floor?

9 ft

8 ft   _____9 × 8_____ = _____ sq ft

4 Mrs. Jones made a new curtain for 1 window. The window is 3 feet wide and 5 feet tall. How much cloth did she use?

3 ft

5 ft   _____ = _____ sq ft

Name _____

Area and Volume

90

⭐ The **volume** of a shape is the amount of space inside the shape or how much it can hold. Find the volume of a rectangular figure by multiplying the length times the width by the depth.

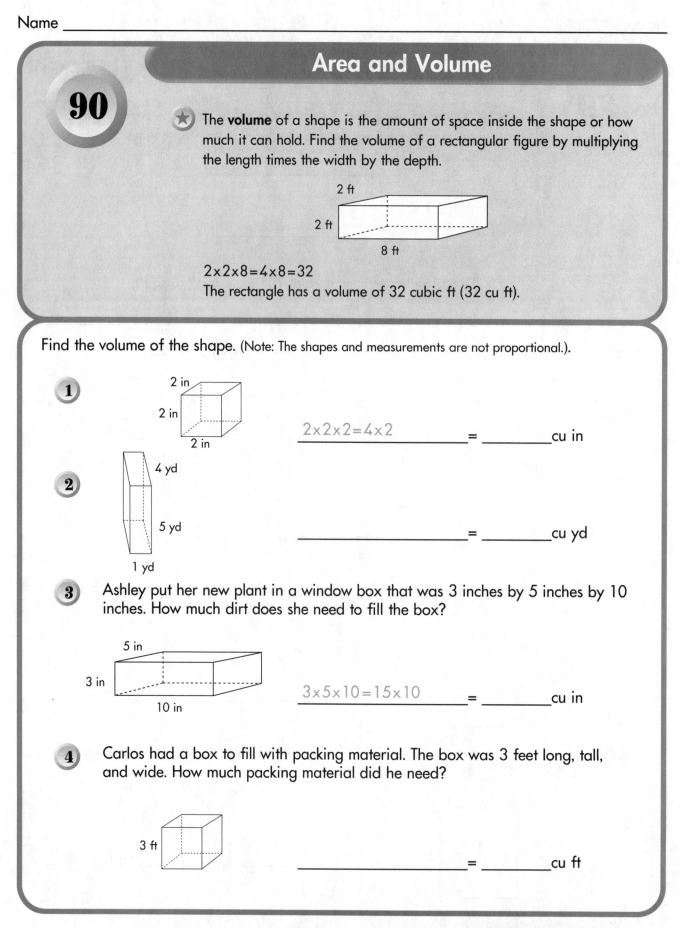

2 ft
2 ft
8 ft

$2 \times 2 \times 8 = 4 \times 8 = 32$
The rectangle has a volume of 32 cubic ft (32 cu ft).

Find the volume of the shape. (Note: The shapes and measurements are not proportional.).

1

2 in
2 in
2 in

$2 \times 2 \times 2 = 4 \times 2$ _____ = _____ cu in

2

4 yd
5 yd
1 yd

_____ = _____ cu yd

3 Ashley put her new plant in a window box that was 3 inches by 5 inches by 10 inches. How much dirt does she need to fill the box?

5 in
3 in
10 in

$3 \times 5 \times 10 = 15 \times 10$ _____ = _____ cu in

4 Carlos had a box to fill with packing material. The box was 3 feet long, tall, and wide. How much packing material did he need?

3 ft

_____ = _____ cu ft

Name _____

Take a Test Drive

Fill in the bubble beside the correct answer.

1 Which of these is a right angle?

○ ○ ○ ○

2 How long is the side marked *x*?

3 in
2 in   x
3 in

○ 1 foot
○ 2 inches
○ 3 inches
○ 3 feet

3 What is the name of this figure?

2 in 2 in
2 in

○ pyramid
○ isosceles triangle
○ equilateral triangle
○ prism

4 Which shape is a sphere?

○   ○

○   ○

5 Which shape could not have a square as part of it?

○ pyramid
○ cube
○ cone
○ prism

6 When you measure how wide a shape is, what are you measuring?

○ time
○ length
○ weight
○ volume

7 What is this shape?

○ rectangle
○ square
○ prism
○ cube

8 Which is a measure of weight?

○ inches
○ feet
○ weeks
○ pounds

Name _____

Take a Test Drive

Fill in the bubble beside the correct answer.

1 What would you use to measure your shoelace?

- ○ inches
- ○ feet
- ○ yards
- ○ miles

2 How long is the worm?

- ○ 3 inches
- ○ 3 ½ inches
- ○ 2 ½ feet
- ○ 4 feet

IN. 1 2 3 4

3 About how long is the string?

- ○ 1 ½ inches
- ○ 2 inches
- ○ 2 ½ inches
- ○ 3 inches

IN. 1 2 3 4

4 Which shows how to find the perimeter of the shape?

4 ft ⟋⟍ 4 ft
3 ft

- ○ 4+3=7 feet
- ○ 4+3+4=11 feet
- ○ 4x3=12 square feet
- ○ 4x3x4=48 cubic feet

5 Which shows how to find the area of the shape?

2 in
3 in

- ○ 3+2=5 inches
- ○ 3+2+3+2=10 inches
- ○ 3x2=6 square inches
- ○ 3x2x3=18 cubic inches

6 Which shows how to find the volume of the shape?

3 ft
2 ft
4 ft

- ○ 2+4+3=9 feet
- ○ 2x3=6 square feet
- ○ 2x3x4=24 cubic feet
- ○ 2x3x3=18 cubic feet

7 Brian's fish tank is 10 inches by 5 inches by 8 inches. What does he need to measure to find out how much water he needs to fill his tank?

- ○ length
- ○ perimeter
- ○ area
- ○ volume

8 Dana made a blanket to cover her dog's bed. The bed is 20 inches long and 15 inches wide. How big must the blanket be?

- ○ 5 feet
- ○ 35 square inches
- ○ 300 inches
- ○ 300 square inches

Read Graphs and Tables

★ Tables are easy ways to list information. Titles and headings help you know what numbers stand for.

MoviePlex Schedule

Movie	Theater	Show Times
MegaMan	1	3:30, 6:00, 8:30
Motorcycle Mouse	2	4:15, 6:15, 8:15
Monkey Madness	3	4:00, 6:15, 8:30
Miss Macaroni	4	3:45, 5:30, 7:15

To find what movies are playing at the MoviePlex, look in the column marked **Movie**. The rows give information about where and when each movie is playing.

Use information from the table to answer the questions.

1 If you were in theater 3, what movie would you be seeing?

_____

2 At what times can you see the movie *Miss Macaroni*?

_____

3 What 2 movies begin at 8:30?

_____

4 If you couldn't get to MoviePlex until after 8:00, what movies could you still see?

_____

5 Which movie is the shortest? (Hint: Find the difference between the show times for each movie

to see about how long it is.) _____

6 Which movie is the longest? _____

Read Graphs and Tables

94

⭐ Pictographs use pictures to give information. Sometimes a symbol in a graph stands for more than 1. Each 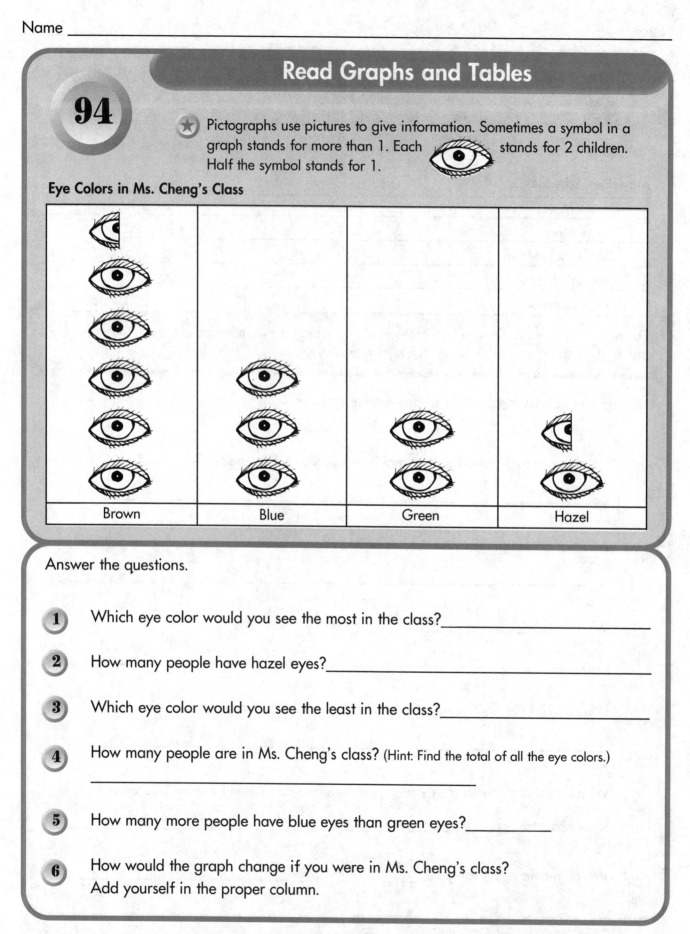 stands for 2 children. Half the symbol stands for 1.

Eye Colors in Ms. Cheng's Class

Brown	Blue	Green	Hazel

Answer the questions.

1. Which eye color would you see the most in the class?_____

2. How many people have hazel eyes?_____

3. Which eye color would you see the least in the class?_____

4. How many people are in Ms. Cheng's class? (Hint: Find the total of all the eye colors.)
   _____

5. How many more people have blue eyes than green eyes?_____

6. How would the graph change if you were in Ms. Cheng's class?
   Add yourself in the proper column.

Create Graphs

95

⭐ A bar graph shows numbers with colored bars. Look at the picture of the pet store. Notice that there are 3 birds in the picture. The bar graph also shows that the pet store has 3 birds.

Fill in the graph using the picture.

Animals for Sale

	1	2	3	4	5	6	7	8
Birds	▓	▓	▓					
Fish								
Rabbits								
Cats								
Dogs								
Snakes								

Create Graphs

96

⭐ Line graphs show change over time. Look at the table to see how Enola's shadow changed during the day.

Enola's Shadow

Time	Length of Shadow
9:00 a.m.	8 feet
10:00 a.m.	6 feet
11:00 a.m.	3 feet
12:00 p.m.	1 foot
1:00 p.m.	2 feet
2:00 p.m.	3 feet
3:00 p.m.	5 feet
4:00 p.m.	7 feet

Find 9:00 in the graph below. Follow the line up to see the dot at 8 feet. This means that at 9:00, the shadow was 8 feet long. The next dot at 10:00 is at 6 feet. At 10:00, the shadow had shrunk to 6 feet. A line connects the dots to make it easier to see what happened.

Use the information in the table to finish the line graph.

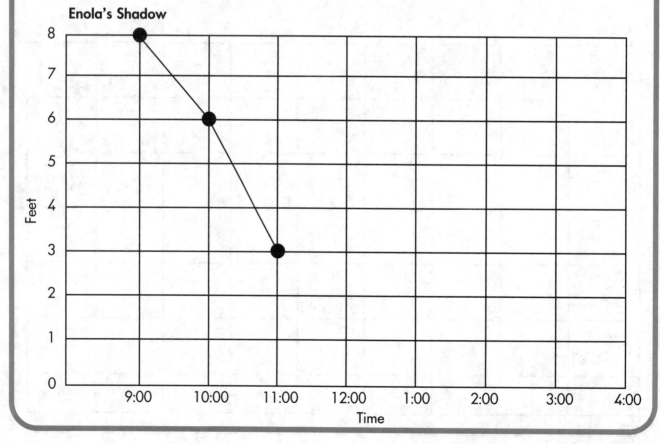

Practice Test

97

Fill in the bubble beside the correct answer.

---

1 What place is the digit 4 in the number 3,468?

- ○ ones
- ○ tens
- ○ hundreds
- ○ thousands

5 Which symbol completes the number sentence?

346 ○ 364

- ○ >
- ○ <
- ○ =
- ○ +

---

2 Which digit is in the ten thousands place in the number 52,041?

- ○ 1
- ○ 2
- ○ 4
- ○ 5

6
57
+34

- ○ 23
- ○ 81
- ○ 83
- ○ 91

---

3 Which expanded form equals 7,032?

- ○ 7 + 0 + 3 + 2
- ○ 700 + 32
- ○ 7,000 + 300 + 2
- ○ 7,000 + 30 + 2

7
485
+224

- ○ 261
- ○ 609
- ○ 709
- ○ 719

---

4 Which number does NOT round to 300?

- ○ 249
- ○ 250
- ○ 311
- ○ 337

8
386
−276

- ○ 10
- ○ 100
- ○ 110
- ○ 662

Name _____

98

Fill in the bubble beside the correct answer.

---

1 Which equation can you use to check the problem?

$$\begin{array}{r} 84 \\ -27 \\ \hline 57 \end{array}$$

○ $\begin{array}{r} 84 \\ +27 \\ \hline 111 \end{array}$ ○ $\begin{array}{r} 57 \\ -27 \\ \hline 30 \end{array}$

○ $\begin{array}{r} 84 \\ +57 \\ \hline 141 \end{array}$ ○ $\begin{array}{r} 27 \\ +57 \\ \hline 84 \end{array}$

5 $\begin{array}{r} 472 \\ -374 \\ \hline \end{array}$

○ 2
○ 98
○ 102
○ 198

---

2 Which pattern shows skip counting by 10?

○ 2, 4, 6, 8, 10
○ 5, 10, 15, 20, 25
○ 10, 20, 30, 40, 50
○ 10, 9, 8, 7, 6

6 $\begin{array}{r} 5 \\ \times 7 \\ \hline \end{array}$

○ 12
○ 25
○ 30
○ 35

---

3 Which does NOT equal 10 divided by 2?

○ $10 \div 2$ ○ $2\overline{)10}$

○ $\dfrac{10}{2}$ ○ 10×2

7 $80 \div 10 =$

○ 0
○ 1
○ 8
○ 10

---

4 Which equation can you use to check the problem?

$$\begin{array}{r} 3 \\ \times 4 \\ \hline 12 \end{array}$$

○ $3 + 4 = 7$
○ $12 - 3 = 9$
○ $12 \div 3 = 4$
○ $3 \times 12 = 36$

8 $15 \div 3 =$

○ 1
○ 2
○ 3
○ 5

Name _____

99

Fill in the bubble beside the correct answer.

1 Which fraction matches the picture?

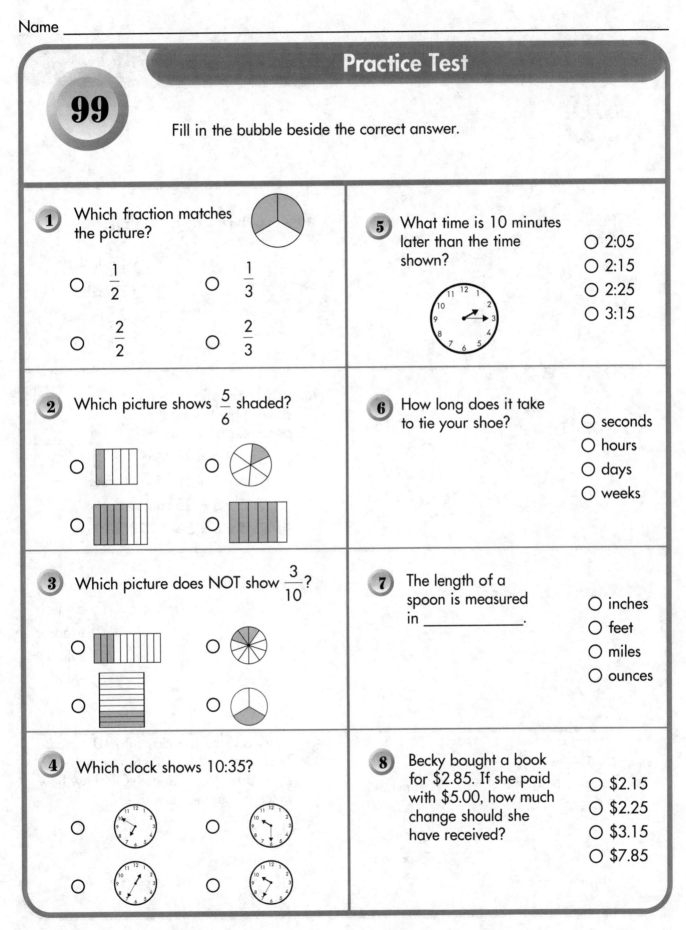

- ○ $\frac{1}{2}$
- ○ $\frac{1}{3}$
- ○ $\frac{2}{2}$
- ○ $\frac{2}{3}$

2 Which picture shows $\frac{5}{6}$ shaded?

- ○
- ○
- ○
- ○

3 Which picture does NOT show $\frac{3}{10}$?

- ○
- ○
- ○
- ○

4 Which clock shows 10:35?

- ○
- ○
- ○
- ○

5 What time is 10 minutes later than the time shown?

- ○ 2:05
- ○ 2:15
- ○ 2:25
- ○ 3:15

6 How long does it take to tie your shoe?

- ○ seconds
- ○ hours
- ○ days
- ○ weeks

7 The length of a spoon is measured in _____.

- ○ inches
- ○ feet
- ○ miles
- ○ ounces

8 Becky bought a book for $2.85. If she paid with $5.00, how much change should she have received?

- ○ $2.15
- ○ $2.25
- ○ $3.15
- ○ $7.85

Name _____

100

Fill in the bubble beside the correct answer.

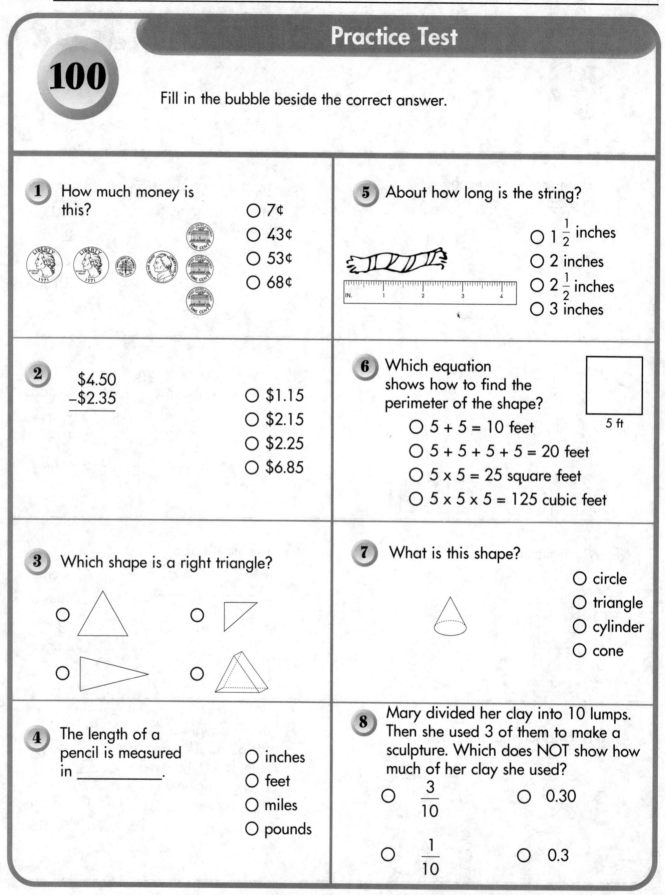

1 How much money is this?

- ○ 7¢
- ○ 43¢
- ○ 53¢
- ○ 68¢

2
$4.50
−$2.35

- ○ $1.15
- ○ $2.15
- ○ $2.25
- ○ $6.85

3 Which shape is a right triangle?

- ○
- ○
- ○
- ○

4 The length of a pencil is measured in _____.

- ○ inches
- ○ feet
- ○ miles
- ○ pounds

5 About how long is the string?

- ○ $1\frac{1}{2}$ inches
- ○ 2 inches
- ○ $2\frac{1}{2}$ inches
- ○ 3 inches

6 Which equation shows how to find the perimeter of the shape?

5 ft

- ○ 5 + 5 = 10 feet
- ○ 5 + 5 + 5 + 5 = 20 feet
- ○ 5 x 5 = 25 square feet
- ○ 5 x 5 x 5 = 125 cubic feet

7 What is this shape?

- ○ circle
- ○ triangle
- ○ cylinder
- ○ cone

8 Mary divided her clay into 10 lumps. Then she used 3 of them to make a sculpture. Which does NOT show how much of her clay she used?

- ○ $\frac{3}{10}$
- ○ 0.30
- ○ $\frac{1}{10}$
- ○ 0.3

Math Grade 3 Tracking Sheet

Activity	Possible	My Score
Unit 1		
1	8	
2	16	
3	16	
4	18	
5	26	
6	19	
7	19	
8	20	
9	24	
10	24	
Test Scores		
11	8	
12	8	
Unit 2		
13	36	
14	36	
15	27	
16	27	
17	20	
18	30	
19	18	
20	30	
Test Scores		
21	8	
22	8	
Unit 3		
23	36	
24	36	
25	27	

Activity	Possible	My Score
26	27	
27	20	
28	30	
29	26	
30	30	
31	20	
32	18	
Test Scores		
33	8	
34	8	
Unit 4		
35	11	
36	12	
37	32	
38	33	
39	32	
40	32	
41	33	
42	33	
43	33	
44	32	
45	33	
46	33	
47	23	
48	23	
49	33	
50	33	
Test Scores		
51	8	
52	8	

Activity	Possible	My Score
Unit 5		
53	12	
54	10	
55	8	
56	8	
57	6	
58	6	
59	8	
60	10	
61	9	
62	4	
Test Scores		
63	8	
64	8	
Unit 6		
65	9	
66	9	
67	9	
68	7	
69	6	
70	6	
71	5	
72	5	
73	7	
74	6	
Test Scores		
75	8	
76	8	
Unit 7		
77	7	

Activity	Possible	My Score
78	6	
79	9	
80	4	
81	6	
82	7	
83	10	
84	16	
85	8	
86	8	
87	4	
88	4	
89	4	
90	4	
Test Scores		
91	8	
92	8	
Unit 8		
93	6	
94	6	
95	5	
96	5	
Test Scores		
97	8	
98	8	
99	8	
100	8	

Math 3 Answer Key

Activity 1
1. 2 hundreds, 3 tens, 6 ones
2. 4 hundreds, 0 tens, 9 ones
3. 0 hundreds, 8 tens, 4 ones
4. 3 hundreds, five tens, 0 ones
5. 624
6. 205
7. 576
8. 320

Activity 2
1. 3,405
2. 2,602
3. 5,264
4. 7,930
5. 8,340
6. 6,053
7. 581
8. 6,421
9. 475
10. 2,009
11. 1,438
12. 502
13. 3,442
14. 714
15. 1,643
16. 411

Activity 3
1. 7,483   461
2. 435   3,227
3. 631   4,068
4. 5,407   122
5. 8,167   706
6. 4,230   4,400
7. 1,000+800+60+3
8. 900+40+2
9. 4,000+700+30
10. 5,000+70+2

Activity 4
1. 10,000+4,000+300+60+7
2. 9,000+200+8
3. 1,000+20+9
4. 500+90+4
Across:
A. 5321
C. 93
E. 4367
G. 159

I. 9200
J. 40
K. 6703
Down:
A. 58
B. 193
D. 3610
E. 442
F. 75
H. 947
I. 906

Activity 5
1. 20 and 30, 20
2. 50 and 60, 60
3. 10   70   0   50
4. 20   70   30   20
5. 90   90   40   20
6. 70   80   40   50

Activity 6
1. 100   800
2. 200   300
3. 400   0
4. 400   500
5. 200   100
6. 500   900   400
7. 700   900   800
8. 100   300   300

Activity 7
1. 3400, 3000   8935, 9000
2. 1587, 2000   2490, 2000
3. 2408, 2000   532, 1000
4. 5372, 5000   464, 0
5. 4850, 5000   1092, 1000
6. 3,000   8,000   6,000
7. 1,000   3,000   1,000
8. 3,000   4,000   7,000

Activity 8
1. 340 and 350, 340
2. 690 and 700, 700
3. 490   100   120
4. 990   150   700
5. 1,400   6,000   8,000
6. 7,600   7,100   4,800
7. 3,800   8,400   2,400
8. 4,600   9,900   5,400

Activity 9
1. >   <   <
2. <   =   <
3. <   <   >
4. <   <   =
5. >   >   <
6. =   >   <
7. <   >   <
8. >   =   >

Activity 10
1. <   >   <
2. =   <   >
3. >   >   <
4. >   <   <
5. >   >   >
Answers will vary.
Sample responses given:
6. 12+12   431   64
7. 371   200+72   908+50
8. 460+9   834   415

Activity 11—Take a Test Drive
1. 325
2. 7 hundreds, no tens, 3 ones
3. 5,860
4. 379
5. 2,056
6. 4,000+800+50
7. 30
8. 0

Activity 12—Take a Test Drive
1. 500
2. 550
3. 4,000
4. 3,600
5. 600
6. <
7. 364
8. >

Activity 13
1. 9   11   14   13
2. 15   14   15   12
3. 14   16   16   10
4. 13   17   14   9   13   12
5. 15   10   13   15   10   14
6. 11   14   12   13   11   8
7. 12   17   11   16   12   18

Activity 14
1. 10 8   18   16
2. 7   14   7   17
3. 14 11   19   9
4. 8   12   17   14   13   15
5. 18 8   16   10   12   11
6. 15 13   18   20   10   13
7. 19 12   16   17   11   15

Activity 15
1. 59 68   99   49   89   89
2. 87 59   87   97   79   71
3. 79 89   87   97   68   79
4. 89 88   85   95   75   87
5. 56 students
6. 78 vegetable sticks
7. 37 miles

Activity 16
1. 539 797 899 196 938 397
2. 497 628 484 989 799 787
3. 287 961 668 817 789 859
4. 694 849 767 974 774 597
5. 298 students
6. 359 cards
7. 387 books

Activity 17
1. 52 yes 37 no   82 yes   98 no
2. 63 yes 79 no   84 yes   61 yes
3. 87 no 61 yes   80 yes   89 no
4. 20 yes 90 yes 81 yes   49 no
5. 93 yes 93 no   90 yes   83 yes

Activity 18
1. 38 91   75   100 43   81
2. 90 30   69   74   63   70
3. 99 74   75   59   250 95
4. 100 99   141 81   121 89
5. 156 97   82   92   86   91

Activity 19
1. 619 tens   799 none
   930 ones, tens 770 ones
2. 712 ones   818 tens
   859 none   509 tens
3. 700 tens   791 ones
   747 none   308 tens
4. 381 382 528 938 394 828

Activity 20
1. 332 760 843 635 971 931
2. 252 774 565 978 641 701
3. 739 635 713 893 900 613

4. 747 759 992 676 702 907
5. 292 911 901 474 927 1008

Activity 21—Take a Test Drive
1. 15
2. 77
3. 89
4. 479
5. 498
6. 569
7. 287
8. 33+27

Activity 22—Take a Test Drive
1. 46+32
2. 60
3. 96
4. 218+530
5. 571
6. 788
7. 725
8. 731

Activity 23
1. 5   9   5   8
2. 9   9   8   6
3. 3   4   8   8
4. 9   3   7   7   10   8
5. 7   4   6   4   6   4
6. 0   7   6   5   5   9
7. 9   7   7   5   1   9

Activity 24
1. 4   9   6   7
2. 8   10   9   2
3. 4   7   3   9
4. 8   5   0   4   9   4
5. 9   8   9   1   8   8
6. 2   9   8   7   5   7
7. 8   6   6   7   9   7

Activity 25
1. 20 12   11   33   34   53
2. 62 22   23   12   19   52
3. 22 21   37   35   71   47
4. 63 10   31   30   71   53
5. 42 cards
6. 32 times more
7. 23 more miles

Activity 26
1. 471 23   322 644 231 141
2. 21 115 232 421 104 120
3. 411 167 453 100 111 304

4. 161 801 150 2   421 203
5. 241 students
6. 22 apples
7. 110 letters

Activity 27
1. 35 yes 12 no   28 yes   29 yes
2. 23 yes 40 no   42 yes   19 yes
3. 9 yes 39 yes 8 yes   28 yes
4. 18 yes 8 yes   36 yes   39 yes
5. 9 yes 34 yes 19 yes   24 yes

Activity 28
1. 26 58   71   48   11   34
2. 78 29   50   23   38   18
3. 19 8   56   22   26   78
4. 25 19   18   16   35   19
5. 48 39   9   12   8   24

Activity 29
1. 274 417 170 530 206 192
2. 454 124 308 261 103 127
3. 347 609 366 98 90 363
4. 409 92 177 695 75 108
5. 250 tickets
6. 105 people

Activity 30
1. 399 231 597 89 208 382
2. 309 329 36 179 89 88
3. 91 78 166 193 251 188
4. 145 445 32 276 248 169
5. 242 472 254 287 246 33

Activity 31
1. 37 + 21 = 58 correct
   61 − 26 = 35 correct
   81 − 34 = 47 incorrect
   4 + 34 = 38 incorrect
2. 83 − 48 = 35 correct
   47 + 6 = 53 correct
   79 − 17 = 62 correct
   32 + 22 = 54 correct
3. 67 − 19 = 48 incorrect
   78 + 12 = 90 incorrect
   89 − 39 = 60 incorrect
   29 + 9 = 38 correct
4. 56 − 45 = 11 correct
   23 + 47 = 70 incorrect
   98 − 36 = 62 incorrect
   76 + 9 = 85 correct
5. 44 − 29 = 15 incorrect
   29 + 18 = 47 correct
   93 − 27 = 66 correct
   39 + 44 = 83 incorrect

Activity 32
1. 118 + 111 = 229 incorrect
   766 − 429 = 337 incorrect
   761 − 238 = 523 correct
   582 + 323 = 905 incorrect
2. 689 − 382 = 307 incorrect
   389 + 96 = 485 correct
   944 − 291 = 653 correct
   269 + 387 = 656 incorrect
3. 899 − 650 = 249 correct
   650 + 186 = 836 incorrect
   741 − 396 = 345 correct
   169 + 109 = 278 correct
4. 979 − 255 = 724 incorrect
   69 + 568 = 637 correct
   317 − 247 = 70 incorrect
   136 + 318 = 454 correct
5. 518 pages
6. 91 miles
7. 678 people

Activity 33—Take a Test Drive
1. 21
2. 34
3. 120
4. 203
5. 53 − 28
6. 348 − 257
7. 15
8. 12

Activity 34—Take a Test Drive
1. 4
2. 38
3. 554
4. 645
5. 299
6. 577
7. 36 + 48 = ?
8. 72 − 44 = 32

Activity 35
1. 8, 10, 12, 14, 16, 18, 20
2. 20, 25, 30, 35, 40, 45, 50
3. 40, 50, 60, 70, 80, 90, 100
4. 12, 15, 18, 21, 24, 27, 30
5. 24, 30, 36, 42, 48, 54, 60
   by 2: 2, 4, 6, 8, 10, 12
   by 3: 3, 6, 9, 12, 15, 18
   by 4: 4, 8, 12, 16, 20, 24
   by 5: 5, 10, 15, 20, 25, 30
   by 6: 6, 12, 18, 24, 30, 36
   by 10: 10, 20, 30, 40, 50, 60

Activity 36
1. 7, 14, 21, 28, 35, 42, 49
2. 8, 16, 24, 32, 40, 48, 56
3. 9, 18, 27, 36, 45, 54, 63
4. 20, 40, 60, 80, 100, 120, 140
5. 25, 50, 75, 100, 125, 150, 175
6. 100, 200, 300, 400, 500, 600, 700
7. 64
8. 88
9. 180
10. 200
11. 1,000
12. 2,000

Activity 37
1. 24 8 14 54 36 35
2. 32 7 4 12 15 40
3. 42 12 72 36 45 8
4. 10 49 30 3 14 56
5. 9 30 8 16 24 48
6. 16 swings
7. 18 cups

Activity 38
1. 24 27 35 81 12 21
2. 64 25 16 18 4 32
3. 48 54 5 36 32 42
4. 10 72 49 20 6 28
5. 3 27 42 2 9 45
6. 21 cookies
7. 40 plants
8. 27 coaches

Activity 39
1. 30 0 4 70 0 10
2. 64 8 6 20 5 0
3. 60 18 4 13 0 15
4. 22 0 6 16 50 0
5. 16 14 90 0 20 12
6. 12 flowers
7. 7 pencils

Activity 40
1. 36 128 490 48 57 320
2. 48 270 35 480 60 126
3. 42 25 255 200 36 210
4. 120 55 420 81 168 96
5. 50 108 560 66 180 40
6. 105 people
7. 120 chalkboards

Activity 41
1. 70 159 405 123 160 546
2. 246 60 288 56 400 88
3. 36 100 74 368 244 102
4. 44 490 69 280 24 72
5. 59 273 420 68 47 180
6. 26 pounds
7. 200 crackers
8. 560 pages

Activity 42
1. 46 108 72 75 56 114
2. 84 102 108 80 100 78
3. 36 98 74 52 108 66
4. 57 96 84 280 75 72
5. 108 68 54 162 112 72
6. 38 pencils
7. 84 peaches
8. 75 days

Activity 43
1. 72 76 81 91 112 95
2. 128 50 114 117 72 78
3. 58 74 92 48 70 60
4. 96 96 92 85 135 72
5. 94 108 84 76 90 54
6. 84 cherries
7. 116 T-shirts
8. 65 stairs

Activity 44
1. 9 3 2 7 4 4
2. 3 9 7 2 6 8
3. 6 5 9 6 2 5
4. 8 3 3 9 7 9
5. 4 8 4 4 5 9
6. 7 cars
7. 7 pages

Activity 45
1. 6 4 3 9 9 6
2. 2 9 7 9 9 4
3. 1 6 5 6 2 7
4. 7 6 4 5 8 1
5. 7 5 9 6 5 3
6. 8 students
7. 8 trees
8. 8 weeks

Activity 46
1. 13 15 9 7 19 6
2. 4 5 3 7 8 6
3. 8 2 10 5 4 1
4. 3 14 9 2 1 6

5. 8 18 20 16 4 17
6. 6 markers
7. 6 balloons
8. 3 slices

Activity 47
1. 24 4 24 6
2. 35 5 35 7
3. 72 8 72 9
4. 15 3 15 5
5. 16 8 16 2
6. 56 pages
7. 12 tricks
8. 30 strawberries

Activity 48
1. 8 48 6 48
2. 3 21 7 21
3. 9 45 5 45
4. 2 18 9 18
5. 8 32 4 32
6. 8 bagels
7. 32 toothbrushes
8. 9 seeds

Activity 49
1. 9 2 3 3 8 6
2. 5 6 4 8 9 8
3. 7 5 4 8 7 2
4. 3 9 7 4 6 9
5. 6 4 4 6 8 7
6. 9 marbles
7. 5 desks
8. 7 students

Activity 50
1. 7 7 5 4 5 3
2. 7 4 9 9 6 5
3. 5 2 5 9 3 8
4. 8 8 6 2 5 2
5. 6 6 9 6 7 8
6. 9 third graders
7. 3 towns
8. 7 fish

Activity 51—Take a Test Drive
1. 3
2. 5, 10, 15, 20, 25
3. 0
4. 16
5. 90
6. 35
7. 7
8. 3

Activity 52—Take a Test Drive
1. 5
2. 4
3. 15 ÷ 3 = 5
4. 4 x 6 = 24
5. $\begin{array}{r}6\\2\overline{)12}\end{array}$
6. 8 ÷ 4 = 2
7. 5
8. 2

Activity 53
1. c
2. f
3. b
4. e
5. d
6. a
7. l
8. g
9. i
10. h
11. k
12. j

Activity 54
1. 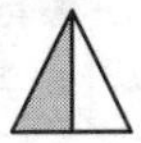 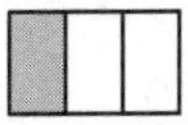
2. 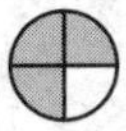 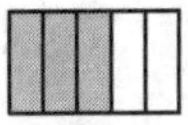
3. 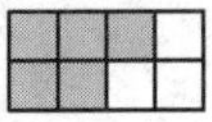 
4.  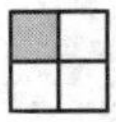
5. 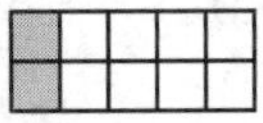 

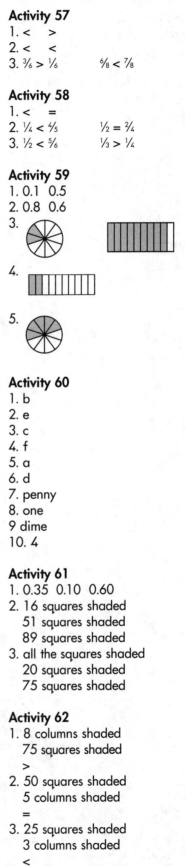

Activity 55
1. $\frac{1}{2}$ $\frac{2}{3}$
2. $\frac{3}{4}$ $\frac{7}{8}$
3. $\frac{1}{6}$ $\frac{2}{2}$
4. $\frac{4}{8}$ $\frac{4}{5}$

Activity 56
1. $\frac{1}{3}$ $\frac{3}{4}$
2. $\frac{1}{2}$ $\frac{3}{8}$
3. $\frac{1}{3}$ $\frac{3}{5}$
4. $\frac{1}{8}$ of the pie
5. $\frac{2}{3}$ of his collection

Activity 57
1. < >
2. < <
3. $\frac{3}{6} > \frac{1}{6}$ $\frac{6}{8} < \frac{7}{8}$

Activity 58
1. < =
2. $\frac{1}{4} < \frac{4}{5}$ $\frac{1}{2} = \frac{2}{4}$
3. $\frac{1}{2} < \frac{5}{6}$ $\frac{1}{3} > \frac{1}{4}$

Activity 59
1. 0.1 0.5
2. 0.8 0.6
3.  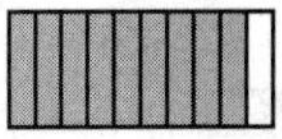
4. 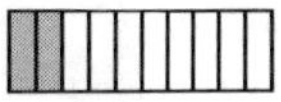
5. 

Activity 60
1. b
2. e
3. c
4. f
5. a
6. d
7. penny
8. one
9 dime
10. 4

Activity 61
1. 0.35 0.10 0.60
2. 16 squares shaded
51 squares shaded
89 squares shaded
3. all the squares shaded
20 squares shaded
75 squares shaded

Activity 62
1. 8 columns shaded
75 squares shaded
>
2. 50 squares shaded
5 columns shaded
=
3. 25 squares shaded
3 columns shaded
<

4. 35 squares shaded
   4 columns shaded
   <

Activity 63—Take a Test Drive
1. ⅔
2. ⅕
3. 3/3
4.
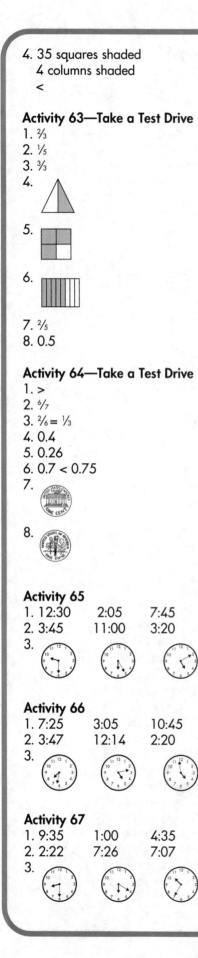
5.
6.
7. ⅖
8. 0.5

Activity 64—Take a Test Drive
1. >
2. 6/7
3. 2/6 = ⅓
4. 0.4
5. 0.26
6. 0.7 < 0.75
7.
8.

Activity 65
1. 12:30   2:05   7:45
2. 3:45   11:00   3:20
3.

Activity 66
1. 7:25   3:05   10:45
2. 3:47   12:14   2:20
3.

Activity 67
1. 9:35   1:00   4:35
2. 2:22   7:26   7:07
3.

Activity 68
1. days
2. seconds
3. minutes
4. weeks
5. seconds
6. years
7. Answers will vary.
   Sample responses are given.
   Do 20 sit-ups, write my name
   and address, run around my
   house, heat something in the
   microwave, toast a piece of
   bread

Activity 69
1. 5, 10, 11 = 11¢
2. 10, 20, 30, 40, 45 = 45¢
3. 25, 35, 40, 41 = 41¢
4. 25, 30, 35, 40, 41, 42 = 42¢
5. 95¢
6. 35¢

Activity 70
1. .25, .50, .75, .85, .95, 1.00,
   1.05, 1.06 = $1.06
2. .25, .50, .75, .80, .81, .82, .83
   = $0.83
3. .25, .50, .75, 1.00, 1.25
   = $1.25
4. .25, .50, .75, 1.00, 1.10, 1.15
   = $1.15
5. $0.45
6. $0.28

Activity 71
1. $15.00 + $4.50 = $19.50
   $4.50 + $3.25 = $7.75
2. $15.00 + $15.00 = $30.00
   $4.50 + 4.50 = $9.00
3. $15.00 + $4.50 + $3.25
   = $22.75
   $3.25 + $3.25 = $6.50
4. $4.50 + $4.50 + $3.25
   = $12.25
   $15.00 + $3.25 = $18.25
5. 1 $5-bill, 2 $1-bills, 3 quarters

Activity 72
1. $0.85 + $0.85 + $0.60
   = $2.30
2. $1.00 + $1.50 + $1.50
   = $4.00
3. $0.85 + $0.60 + $0.60 + $1.50

= $3.55
4. $0.85 + $0.60 + $1.50 + $1.00
   = $3.95
5. 3 $1-bills, 3 quarters, 2 dimes

Activity 73
1. $5.00 − $0.50 = $4.50
2. $5.00 − $1.00 = $4.00
3. $5.00 − $1.35 = $3.65
4. ($1.35 + $1.00 = $2.35)
   $5.00 − $2.35 = $2.65
5. ($1.35 + $0.50 = $1.85)
   $5.00 − $1.85 = $3.15
6. ($1.35 + $1.35 + $0.60 = $3.30)
   $5.00 − $3.30 = $1.70
7. ($0.50 + $0.60 + $1.00 = $2.10)
   $5.00 − $2.10 = $2.90

Activity 74
1. $1.75 + $0.90 = $2.65;
   $3.00 − $2.65 = $0.35
2. $2.00 + $0.75 + $1.05 = $3.80;
   $4.00 − $3.80 = $0.20
3. $1.75 + $2.00 + $1.05 + $0.90
   = $5.70; No, they do not have
   enough money.
4. $5.70 − $5.00 = $0.70;
   They need 70¢ more.
5. $2.00 + $0.75 + $0.90 = $3.65;
   Yes, she has enough money.
6. $4.00 − $3.65 = $0.35 in
   change

Activity 75—Take a Test Drive
1. 2:20
2. 9:42
3.
4. 4:35
5. 10:55
6. minutes
7. years
8. hours

Activity 76—Take a Test Drive
1. 57¢
2.

3. $2.30
4. $4.45
5. $6.96
6. $1.75

7. 49 cents
8. $0.75

Activity 77
1. 3 sides, 3 angles, no right angles
2. 4 sides, 4 angles, yes right angles
3. 4 sides, 4 angles, yes right angles
4. 0 sides, 0 angles, no right angles
5. 5 sides, 5 angles, no right angles
6. 6 sides, 6 angles, no right angles
7. 8 sides, 8 angles, no right angles

Activity 78
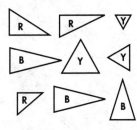

Activity 79
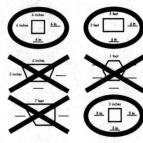

Activity 80
1.
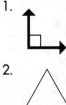
2.
3. 2 inches on each side
4. 13

Activity 81
1. triangles
2. triangles, square
3. squares
4. triangle, circle
5. rectangles
6. circles, rectangle

Activity 82
1. c
2. d
3. e
4. b
5. a
6. f
7.

Activity 83
1. length
2. time
3. weight
4. weight
5. length
6. time
7. length
8. weight
9. 0.5 pound
10. 1 hour and 17 minutes

Activity 84
1. inches   miles
2. feet   feet
3. miles   inches
4. inches   miles
5. centimeters kilometers
6. meters   meters
7. kilometers centimeters
8. centimeters kilometers

Activity 85
1. 1 inch
2. 2 ½ inches
3. 4 inches
4. ½ inch
5. 3 cm
6. 7.5 cm
7. 11 cm
8. 5 cm

Activity 86
1. 1 inch
2. 2 inches
3. 2 inches
4. 3 inches
5. 10 cm
6. 3 cm
7. 8 cm
8. 5 cm

Activity 87
1. 3 + 3 + 2 = 8 ft
2. 1 + 4 + 1 + 4 = 10 yd
3. 10 + 10 + 10 + 10 + 10 = 50 in
4. 4 + 6 + 4 + 6 = 20 ft

Activity 88
1. 1 + 5 + 1 + 5 = 12 feet
2. 9 + 9 + 9 + 9 = 36 inches
3. 8 + 4 + 8 + 4 = 24 yards
4. 15 + 10 + 15 + 10 = 50 feet

Activity 89
1. 2 x 2 = 4 sq in
2. 2 x 5 = 10 sq ft
3. 9 x 8 = 72 sq ft
4. 5 x 3 = 15 sq ft

Activity 90
1. 2 x 2 x 2 = 8 cu in
2. 4 x 5 x 1 = 20 cu yd
3. 3 x 5 x 10 = 150 cu in
4. 3 x 3 x 3 = 27 cu ft

Activity 91—Take a Test Drive
1.

2. 2 inches
3. equilateral triangle
4.

5. cone
6. length
7. cube
8. pounds

Activity 92—Take a Test Drive
1. inches
2. 3 ½ inches
3. 2 inches
4. 4 + 3 + 4 = 11 feet
5. 3 x 2 = 6 square inches
6. 2 x 3 x 4 = 24 cubic feet
7. volume
8. 300 square inches

Activity 93
1. *Monkey Madness*
2. 3:45, 5:30, 7:15
3. *MegaMan* and *Monkey Madness*
4. *MegaMan, Motorcycle Mouse, and Monkey Madness*
5. *Miss Macaroni*
6. *MegaMan*

Activity 94
1. brown
2. 3
3. hazel
4. 24
5. 2
6. Answers will vary.

Activity 95
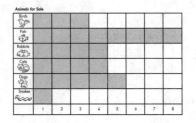

Activity 96
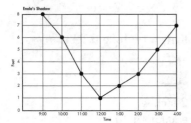

Activity 97—Practice Test
1. hundreds
2. 5
3. 7,000+30+2
4. 249
5. <
6. 91
7. 709
8. 110

Activity 98—Practice Test
1. 27 + 57 = 84
2. 10, 20, 30, 40, 50
3. 10 x 2
4. 12 ÷ 3 = 4
5. 98

6. 35
7. 8
8. 5

Activity 99—Practice Test
1. ⅔
2.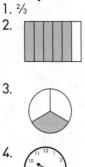

3.

4.

5. 2:25
6. seconds
7. inches
8. $2.15

Activity 100—Practice Test
1. 68¢
2. $2.15
3.

4. inches
5. 2 ½ inches
6. 5 + 5 + 5 + 5 = 20 feet
7. cone
8. ¹⁄₁₀